Elia Benamozegh

Jewish and Christian Ethics With a Criticism on Mahomedism

Elia Benamozegh

Jewish and Christian Ethics With a Criticism on Mahomedism

ISBN/EAN: 9783337027629

Printed in Europe, USA, Canada, Australia, Japan

Cover: Foto ©Lupo / pixelio.de

More available books at **www.hansebooks.com**

JEWISH

CHRISTIAN ETHICS

CRITICISM ON MAHOMEDISM

BENAMOZEGH.

TRANSLATOR'S PREFACE.

And ye (Israel) are my witnesses. Is there a God besides me? Yea, there is no Rock, I know none.—Isaiah, xliv. 8.

THE most effective method of counteracting an old and wide-spread error, is to show *how* and *why* it arose. Although a logical refutation, *a priori*, or an historical one from cause and effect, *a posteriori*, would have more weight with the thinker or lover of abstract ideas, yet, for the majority at least, no method seems better than the first. Both the latter indeed are admirably used in the fine essay here presented to the reader, and the author ostensibly rests his case upon their provings; yet the whole tenor of his discourse undesignedly evolves the first in a remarkable degree. The *reason of the origin* of Christianity clearly comes out, and the splendor of those ethereal doctrines that it claims as its own, are traced in detail and with unerring accuracy to their true source—the then setting sun of Judaism. Even the real *peculiarities* of the new system, such as *Justification by Faith, Freedom from the Law*, &c., are ably shown to be misapplications of old Rabbinical doctrines or traditions.

We have had, within the past half century, many works exposing the delusions from which Christianity sprung; none of these, however, occupies exclusively that portion of the field of inquiry explored by this essay, chiefly, we suppose, because the writers lacked that knowledge of *Hebrew* literature, of the Talmud, and the still more recondite Cabalistic works with which Jews alone are conversant. As this essay was written by one well versed in Hebrew lore, all the necessary arguments are brought to bear,—*necessary* we say; for as a comparison is here made between an original creed (Judaism) and its two main derivative branches (Christianity and Mohammedanism), it is obvious it could not have been instituted without a full acquaintance with the former.

In the second chapter are given an analysis of the extraordinary doctrines taught by Paul, of the Hebrew doctrines from which he manufactured his seductive fictions, and the consequences, obvious as well as inevitable, which they at once and for centuries produced. This portion of the book is highly curious and interesting. We would also call special attention to the ninth chapter, where the *universal* and *cosmopolitan* character of Judaism is vindicated.

The main argument of the book is that Judaism has a two-fold character—a material and a spiritual side; the first, dealing with man's worldly interests and his various relations to the present world; the second, with the conscience of the individual, with things most real indeed, but unseen or to come: and that this system—true to nature, true to the necessities of man's constitution and of his present state—has been "bisected" and therefore wholly marred by the two offshoots herein criticised. Christianity, it is shown, has taken the spiritual side of Judaism, and insisting upon this alone to the exclusion of the other (so indispensable in man's present state), has made itself thereby ridiculously impracticable, and created not only the wildest fanaticism but—whenever it has had full play, unchecked by reason or common sense—the most revolting licentiousness. Mohammedanism, on the other hand, ignoring Judaism's etherial side, has adopted as its sole canon the secular part of the Mosaic Code— given solely for the preservation of the state and of society; hence the materialism, the torpor of the spiritual and purifying element in man's nature, and the social and political semi-barbarism so observable in Islamism. Still, a system springing from the latter selection, must obviously be preferable in theory and practice; in theory, as it strictly preserved the Monotheism of its mother-creed, and never gave to a creature the incommunicable attributes of the First Cause; and in practice, as it would not be liable to fall into the extravagances of its "*solely-spiritual*" sister-creed. All this is shown with great ability by the author.

So far, in this exclusive adoption of a special side of Judaism, can we draw a parallel between the two systems: but then (unfortunately for Christianity) they remarkably diverge; for while Islamism, as shown in the second part, transcribes exactly, even in their minutiæ, its dogmas and precepts from Judaism, Christianity—as embodied in the Papacy, its most legitimate offspring—has taken nearly all its ceremonials, and most of its practical ordinances, as monasticism, celibacy, auricular confession, pictures, beads, canonization of saints, etc., and some of its dogmas even, as the Lamb, the Trinity, the Immaculate Conception, etc., from Indian creeds, especially from Buddhism. Catholicism is, indeed, so close a copy of the latter, that a disciple of Budda could not without difficulty distinguish one from the other. Protestantism has been a revolt from this amalgamation; but rejecting tradition, that served as a check in some degree upon the fanaticism so native to the soil of Christianity, and encountering in the written records the conflicting and irreconcilable doctrines of Jesus and his apostles, it was naturally rent, like the primitive Church, into a thousand pieces.

Incidentally, this work establishes beyond a doubt two main facts as to the founder of Christianity: the first, that he was in its truest sense, *a fanatic, i. e.* a one-sided philosopher; the second, that he was a *false prophet* (unconsciously perhaps) by asserting that the *end of the world was at hand* (Luke xxi, 32:); to which last we must chiefly ascribe (as the essay shows) the recklessness and vice of the primitive Churches.

The prevailing tone of the work is critical and logical; philosophical, too, at need, yet without a dull or tiresome page. It sparkles sometimes with anecdotes, and is quite free from spleen or bitterness, a condemnation of doctrine never being made the ground of an aspersion of character. Every allowance that reason suggests is made for the errors and short-comings of Jesus and Paul. On the whole, we think, that no *candid Christian* can rise from the perusal of this work without feeling a load lifted from his mind and heart, and without being completely satisfied that, as to the comparative merit of Judaism and Christianity, he has had full and most reliable data for forming or rectifying his judgment.

As the word "Lord" was in a few instances injudiciously employed by the essayist, it did not occur to the translator to alter the term till too late. There is a frequent misuse of the term *Lord* throughout the James' version of the so-called Old Testament. The proper rendering of the original four-letter word (Tetragrammaton), implying past, present and future, would have been the "Eternal." This remark seems needful for Christians, who—accustomed to the application of *Lord* to Jesus in the "New Testament," and reading the captions of the English translators to the books of Prophets, (so ridiculously misleading as to the persons or events therein referred to)—are much more liable to fall into error; nor will it seem trivial to those conversant with Hebrew literature, so sensitive as to any infringement of the first commandment. So we read:

I, I am the Eternal, and besides me there is no *Saviour*.—Isaiah xliii, 11.

TABLE OF CONTENTS.

PART FIRST.

I.

GENERAL REMARKS.

Examination of the Pretensions of Christian Ethics over Philosophy and Paganism.—Its Alleged Superiority to Judaism, and the Absurdity of this Assumption.—Immutability of Divine Declarations; Man capable of Perfection only when the Word of God is Perfect.—A Revelation Repeated is Suspicious and Useless; It Militates against Christianity.—Dissimilarity of Judaism; Its Civil and Moral Polity.—The Requisites of every Government; Christianity Incapable of Fulfilling them.—Patriotism a Jewish Sentiment.—Two ways of Interpreting Fraternity and Universal Equality in Christianity.—Defects and Weakness of Christian Ethics.—The limits of Comparison between both Systems. . . . . 1—12

II.

THE DOCTRINES UPON WHICH THE CHRISTIAN CODE OF MORALS IS FOUNDED.

Abolition of the Law.—How it is understood by Jesus.—Faith without Works.—Rupture between Catholicism and Protestantism.—With Paul, Faith, without Works, Saves.—Contempt for the Body; Mysticism.—It ends in Immorality and Materialism; Proofs from Reason and History.—Gnosticism and its Excesses; Its Seed in the Gospel.—The Spiritualism of Paul, what.—The Liberty of Spiritual Death.—The Faithful, dead in Jesus Christ; Origin of this Fiction.—They rise with Him; Another Fiction, its Origin and Effects upon Morality.—The Redemption.—"The Law, the cause of Sin."—The Redemption of the Jew, the Christian. . . . . 12—29

III.

HISTORICAL RESULTS.

Scandals in the Church.—Embarrassment of the Apostles.—The Nicolites.—The Prophecy of Thyadira.—The Simonians.—Other Gnostic Sects.—Sects of the Middle Ages.—Principles of Gnostic Immorality; Inferential Theory.—Judaism Knows Nothing Similar.—Solitary Exception Confirmatory of our System.—Protestantism and its Ethical Systems.—Quietism. 29—37

IV.

CHRISTIAN ETHICS.

Its Trials and its Pretentions.—Why Hebrew Ethics has not been duly appreciated.—Division of Ethics.—Dignity of Man, his Fall, his Regeneration.—Free Judgment and Grace.—Life.—General Maxims.—Pharisaical Plan.—Examples.—Testimony of the Gospels. . . . .

V.

HUMILITY.

Abraham and Moses.—The Bible.—The "Poor in Spirit."—The Kingdom and the Earth that are to be their Heritage.—Cabalistic Sense necessary for the Comprehension of the Law.—Greatness of the Humble.—Authority.—Example of Jesus.—Submission to Injury.—Other Beatitudes.—The Persecuted.—Pride.—Anger.—Serpent and Dove.—The Child.—Self-Denial.—Voluntary Poverty. . . . . 51—61

VI.

CHARITY.

Accusations of Jesus.—They Strike at the Bible as well as well as at the Pharisees.—Civil Law and Moral Law; Necessity of Distinguishing.—Cupidity and Anger Condemned by the Pharisees.—Their Expansion of the Decalogue.—Supposed Superiority of Gospel Charity.—God is Charity.—Hebrew Charity; Distinct from Alms which it Excludes.—The Three Enemies.—Who the Enemy According to the Gospel.—Country and Society in Christianity.—Parable of the Samaritan. . . . . . 62—75

VII.

UNIVERSAL CHARITY.

Qualities of the Universal Charity of Judaism.—Not to be found in Christian Charity.—Unity of Man's Origin.—The Worth and Results of the Doctrine in the Teachings of the Pharisees.—Man made after God's Image; Value of the Doctrine.—Unity of Destiny.—Moses and Sophonias.—History of the Primitive Ages.—Humanitarian Character of the Prophecies; Can be traced in the Laws.—Justice and Charity equal for all.—Universal Charity of the Pharisees.—Circumstances that Enhance its Value.—Salvation to all Men.—Idea of Man.—Humanitarian Ideas of the Pharisees.—Gentile Greatness equal to that of the High Priest.—Universal Love, Respect for Life, Property, and Reputation.—Restrictions.—Political Enemy.—Christ has Created the Religious Enemy. . . . . 75—85

VIII.

PERSONAL ENEMIES.

Mosaic Precepts and Pharisaical Interpretations.—Forgiveness of Injuries.—Moses, the Prophets, and the Pharisees.—Reward of Pardon.—The Pardon of God.—Duties of the Injurer; Those of the Injured.—Examples of the Pharisees.—What enhances their Morality. . . . . 85—93

IX.

LOVE TO SINNERS.

Meaning of the Pharisees' Reproach to Jesus.—Passage from Ezekiel.—Pharisees Interpretation.—Brotherly Reproof; Its Different Forms.—Aaron the Model of a Priest.—Abraham the Model of Apostles.—Doctors strive to convert Sinners.—Testimony of the Gospels.—Privileges of the Converted.—The Gentiles.—Measure for Measure.—Universality of Judaism. . . 93—103

X.

TRUST IN GOD.

Trust Preached by Jesus.—Its Extravagance.—Two Pharisaical Schools.—The Jewish Prototypes of the Gospel Trust.—The Dogmatic Fiction, Making Man free from Toil.—Toil in Judaism and in Christianity.—Pharisaical Examples.—The Object of Life; *The Glory of God.*—Our Method of Comparing the Two Systems of Morality.—Judgment of Mr. Salvador.—Its Inaccuracy.—His Mode of Characterizing the Systems.—Man Woman.—The House and the Cloister. . . . . . . 104—113

PART SECOND.

ISLAMISM.

MOHAMMEDISM—Its Doctrines. . . . . 1—17
        Worship and Ethics. . . . . 17—23

JEWISH AND CHRISTIAN ETHICS.

CHAPTER I.

EXAMINATION OF THE PRETENSIONS OF CHRISTIAN ETHICS OVER PHILOSOPHY AND PAGANISM—ITS ALLEGED SUPERIORITY TO JUDAISM, AND THE ABSURDITY OF THIS ASSUMPTION—IMMUTABILITY OF DIVINE DECLARATIONS; MAN CAPABLE OF PERFECTION ONLY WHEN THE WORD OF GOD IS PERFECT—A REVELATION REPEATED IS SUSPICIOUS AND USELESS; IT MILITATES AGAINST CHRISTIANITY—DISSIMILARITY OF JUDAISM; ITS CIVIL AND MORAL POLITY—THE REQUISITES OF EVERY GOVERNMENT; CHRISTIANITY INCAPABLE OF FULFILLING THEM—PATRIOTISM A JEWISH SENTIMENT—TWO WAYS OF INTERPRETING FRATERNITY AND UNIVERSAL EQUALITY IN CHRISTIANITY—DEFECTS AND WEAKNESS OF CHRISTIAN ETHICS—THE LIMITS OF COMPARISON BETWEEN BOTH SYSTEMS.

Of all the elements that have aided, in **ancient** or modern times, the triumph of Christianity, the most important, unquestionably, is its *Ethics*. Christianity entertains **so high** an idea of its own moral code, that it does not hesitate to assert, that the absolute excellence of this code is the **best** proof of its own divine origin. **If this** pretention is just, **then** must its Ethics be superior, not **only to** the best products, in this sphere, of the Pagan world, **as well** as to all that human reason could ever produce, but also to **all** that *divine reason* has ever communicated in this respect to the most excellent of mankind. For the divine origin of Christianity cannot be proved, without first **showing** that neither Paganism, Philosophy, nor even Judaism **itself, was** ever able to attain a similar height; which implies, **as far as the** last is concerned, a maturing process, in its **manifestations** at least, of Divine reason.

Are these assumptions,—is this pride of superiority well founded? **Is** there no exaggeration in the praise Christianity lavishes upon itself?

We do not undertake to examine its relations to Paganism, or even to Philosophy. Were such our aim, it would be easy for us, book in hand, to show, that, as to Philosophy, little have the pages of Plato, little the maxims of the Stoics—specially of Epictetus and Marcus Aurelius, the friends of Rabbi Jehudah Hannassi—little the eloquent passages of Cicero, not to mention the noble things Philosophy has produced, and may still produce in ages to come,—to envy in the finest ethical claims put forth by Christianity. As to Paganism, without urging the simplicity, beauty, and elevation of Greco-Roman poetry or theology, we should have to cite only from some sacred book of the East, from Confucius or Menu for instance, to show what man can extract from that rich and inexhaustible soil of divine gift, viz., the religious sentiment.

But what directly concerns us is the superiority that Christianity arrogates to itself over Judaism, and the inferiority in point of Ethics that it ascribes to the latter, inferring therefrom, that it owes this nothing, and that it has reached, by a spontaneous soar alone, so unprecedented an elevation. As long as these assumptions aimed merely to depreciate Pagan morality, they were, we must confess, in a great measure justifiable. If, as we have just said, Pagan religion and philosophy sometimes exaggerated their deserts, their Ethics always lacked that *certainty, purity, elevation,* and *independence,* which were the heritage of Judaism, and of which Christianity afterwards partook. The Ethics of Paganism was not *certain,* because its theology, so far from acquiring influence over minds, missed it rather, by exhibiting its Gods constantly at variance with their own maxims; it was not *pure,* because the vilest interests were its usual incentives to action ; it was not *elevated,* because its views and aspirations did not transcend the horizon of this life ; it was not *independent,* because, merged at one time in the State, in Politics,—at another, enslaved by or interwoven with these, it was hampered by obstacles that continually stopped its free development. These defects Christianity partly removed, at one time falling short of Hebrew morality, at another, urging the anti-Pagan reaction beyond its proper limits, and injuring itself by such fanaticism and excessive austerity. But finally this religion made morality and humanity take a great spring; it overturned the altars that were still reeking with innocent blood, closed the dens where prostitution was regarded as a sacred duty, proclaimed the common origin and universal brotherhood of mankind, effaced the brands that egotism, pride, brute force and wealth had put on the brow of the poor, the unhappy, the conquered and the slave. These benefits and many others are imperishable claims to the respect and gratitude of mankind : Judaism finds here her true reflection, and glories in such manifestations; she admires those devoted children, who issuing from her fold, filled with her spirit, inflamed with **that** zeal which made the Pharisees scour "sea and **land to make one** proselyte,"* have—not brought as they **boast the era** of the Messiah, far from that, but—smoothed the way **for** his advent and heralded his reign. Yes, the Syna**gogue** admires them, and, though crushed by the hand of the **Church,** has not ceased to declare it, especially by the **tongue of** Maimonides. These real merits of Christianity have served **as a** base for enormous pretensions. Without justice, without logic, its Ethics has been declared superior to the Hebrew. Christianity itself, with a wonderful blindness, has given a free rein to prejudice, and permitted the worship of this intoxicating incense; nay! it has formally instituted a comparison between both systems, between the Ethics of Moses and Jesus, and has struggled, as in a medical or legal competition, to show the superiority of its receipts to those of its rival. A singular and instructive spectacle! for if, according to Christian assertion, the excellence of Christian Ethics proves its divine origin, its pretensions lead us back to the lowest earthly regions. For a divine ethical system, a natural sequence to Judaism, would never have parted itself into two orders or degrees; it would never have said: "You have heard what was told to past generations, but I tell you, etc.;" for this *one* God would have been ever conscious of his own identity, and therefore ever consistent in thought, will, and laws.

This is not the only internal contradiction arising from these pretensions. Here, as elsewhere, we have but to express what will suggest itself to the mind of all,—has Christianity any other base than that of Judaism? Is it that each has a different God, a different will, a different authority? Or would evangelical Christianity adopt the doctrine of Marcion (far more reasonable, as we shall hereafter see, than its own), which has **made** of the God of the Jews and of the God of the Christians **two** beings, two wills, two laws, in constant antagonism? No; for evangelical Christianity both gods are identical; it is but one will expressing itself by two different instruments. Now, can God be superior to God? Can the Immutable have now one will, now another? Can he impose laws in different approximations to perfection? And must not any declaration of his will, when once made, **be** consistent with every other expression? Now, according to **the** admission of Christianity, God has spoken to the patriarchs, to Moses, and given them a system of Ethics

* Matt. xxiii. 15.

absolutely perfect, because nothing less than that could emanate from God; otherwise he, too, would be subject to time, accident, and change. But we are told that man is not capable of reaching at a bound the heights of perfection, and that he is essentially a creature of progress. Yes, we reply, and it is for that very reason, and in order that man may attain perfection that God's word is perfect. Man strives to realize it step by step. Like the external world, that issues from God, consisting of imperishable elements, so the second creation, the ideal world, *his word*, issues from him perfect and complete. It falls like the first, amid the accidents of time, the fate and conditions of which it partakes. It hides, like the first, in its inmost depths, unknown power for man's discovery, and permits him to realize only by degrees its beauties and its wealth. But both creations, perfect in themselves, are progressive only as regards their realization. No; the law of God is not progressive, and man, on the other hand, is so only because it is perfect. How, indeed, can we conceive progression without an ideally perfect law, the successive realization of whose traits constitutes progress? What idea can we have of *evolution* without a starting point and goal,—of a work, without a plan or theory?

Now what has Christianity substituted for the God of the Jews, the First-and-the-Last,* the author of the beginning and end of man and of the world? It has ascribed progression to God himself, at least to his *external word;* asserting that this last bends to circumstances, to custom, even to the weakness of man,—has ascribed to him the flexibility of Paul (who is a Jew to Jews and a Gentile to Gentiles), and the base concessions of Jesuits to idolators; it has made a god after its own image, like the gods of Homer, instead of making man after the image of God, as Moses teaches. Thus it not only violates common sense (which can ascribe to Deity but one *will*) but it makes all revelation useless, and by establishing a principle that recoils against itself and imperils each moment its existence, saps its own foundation. With such a theory how could any revelation be necessary? Tell us of a revelation (worthy of the name) that comes to teach man truth he could not otherwise learn, to give him a theory of moral government and virtue which his unassisted reason could not originate,—and this very reason shall bow before it, because the mark of its divine origin will be apparent. But a different revelation,—one that only follows step by step the natural developments of man's powers, and that, instead of uttering at once its final word even at the risk

* Isaiah xliv. 6.

of being misunderstood, doles out eternal truth as the mind and heart are disposed to receive it—such a revelation I say would be at the outset a very suspicious one to a sagacious critic, and above all would be altogether needless as having naught to tell men that they could not tell themselves.

Much more; it is in Jewish revelation that we find the titles, promises, and prophecies upon which Christianity is based. Now, what assurance have we that some social, mental, or moral change in man will not require different methods, different laws,—and that the Messianic promises will not be in their turn obliterated? And even though they should be verified in Christianity (which, let us suppose, fulfilled the prophecies), can it pretend to arrest forever the progress of the world?—to have exhausted the divine wisdom and fertility, and consigned God's word to an eternal silence?—to have closed, for its special benefit, the epochs of revelation?

This Mosaic law, whose permanence seemed foreshadowed by so many miracles, so many resources, has been supplanted you say by another law, another covenant, of which it was but the shadow and forerunner. What tells us that this latter is not likewise a type of and preparation for a purer religion? Is it because God is exhausted? Or because man has changed his nature? Is it because he has no more social, moral, or intellectual changes, through which to pass? Shall the need of a new revelation, manifesting itself a little more than ten centuries after the first, never again show itself in twenty, thirty, or even fifty centuries after the Gospel? To maintain this is impossible. There is a word which Christianity by its assumption of superiority has attached forever to its existence, to its role in the world; there is a name, which, after centuries, has become the mark of the greatest schism, the greatest rupture that the Church has as yet undergone—namely PROTESTANTISM. But it was Christianity that introduced this very Protestantism into the world by establishing a principle which, from age to age, has recoiled upon itself, and which shall one day open the door to another Christianity, another Messiah. For in the hands of God, evil works its own cure. In short, the Church has had and will have Protestants, only because she herself first protested against Judaism.

So we see Christianity cannot claim a morality superior to that of Judaism without wounding its own dearest interest, violating logic, and crumbling the very bases upon which are founded all religion and all morality. Let us, however, descend from these high abstractions, **where Truth,** though more brilliant, is, by reason of this very elevation, less tangible for ordinary minds. Let us institute, if possible, a comparison, fixing its conditions and limits, and let us see in the detail— if it be from its own root that Christianity has drawn its ethics,—its chief claim to the esteem of mankind;—or if it be not rather the natal surroundings, the religion in which it is rooted that supplied it with the principles and elements which were, alas! but too soon forgotten.

A question at the outset presents itself; and, although it may appear at first sight a little strange, we must not neglect it, full sure that its importance will be at once admitted. Are we, in the present comparison, about to compare one system of Ethics with another? Have we here two homogeneous terms that can be weighed in the same balance so that the worth of each can be estimated. This consideration is clearly of great importance. If it were true that, in comparing Judaism with Christianity (as has been the uniform custom), two systems, two principles, of totally different characters, were compared, and that a mere system of Ethics (Christianity), were weighed against a system of Ethics and of Politics combined, or rather against the latter exclusively, no one could maintain that the verdict, whatever it might be, could be just. Now I ask, is it not this precisely that has been hitherto done? Except some few who have made allowance—and that an inadequate one—for this two-fold character of the Mosaic law, all, both friends and foes, have merely taken the book of Moses in one hand and the Gospel in the other, and pronounced to which the palm of superiority should be awarded. Nevertheless, all recognize in Judaism two things very distinct as regards the nature, object and means of each; that it consists of a civil as well as a moral code. Doubtless, there is unity in Judaism; its civil code blends in a thousand ways with its moral one, borrowing sometimes the language of the latter, sometimes adorning itself with its holy splendor. Doubtless too, its Ethics serves not only to purify, enlighten and satisfy the conscience,—to make good citizens for the heavenly Jerusalem,—but also good patriots, good Israelites, good citizens for the earthly Jerusalem. And, in short, there doubtless exists between both systems a continual interchange of service, a reciprocity highly useful to both. But just as it would be indiscreet to separate these in their practical working at Jerusalem, so it would be unjust to confound them in a theoretic examination, especially when face to face with an ethical system, which not only has nothing to do with, but even repudiates politics, and is its most formidable living adversary. It is then, only strict justice, to distinguish well the ethics of Judaism from its politics; the civil code from the religious; the citizen from the Monotheist; or—to express this difference by two names equally dear to God's people—the Jew from the Hebrew, the member of a state government by the Judaic dynasty from the Hebrew, the son of Abraham, the disciple and follower of his faith.* Through not understanding this truth, the Christian Ethics has been judged superior to that of the Jews, or rather to their politics. Could it be otherwise? Could a system of civil government, however pure, however just, ever compete with a system of abstract morality? Could the duties of a nation be framed upon those of an individual, or could international law be ever successfully supplanted by the "Imitation of Christ?" I shall cite but one striking example of this self-evident truth, viz., the forgiveness of injuries,—the very one through which Christianity is thought to approach perfection. Now, try to apply this principle to nations; lay before them those precepts of humility, forbearance, patience and long suffering that so abound in the Gospel; tell them, if you dare, to allow their cheeks to be smitten, to be spit upon, to swallow in silence, and even to requite with benefits the most atrocious injuries—deeds the most sanguinary—and see if a nation can maintain itself with such a code, if invasion, conquest, slavery, and annihilation will not be at once the inevitable consequence? No! If a country or state must live, if nationality be not an empty term, the moral code of the Gospel can never be the law of nations. And why? Because a nation has less duties than an individual; because the number of its duties always diminish as the body politic expands; being for a family less than for an individual; for town less than for a family, for a state less than for a single town, and less for all mankind than for any single state. For each of these different centres owes allegiance only to its superior; humanity, for example, has duties only to its God; to naught else should it bend or subordinate itself. Now, if a nation has a right to exist, if its duties consist precisely in disregarding the Ethics of an individual (in its extreme consequences at least), if Israel lay under the same necessities as every other nation and under far greater ones still, (encompassed as it was by ignorance, injustice and barbarism), if it was in this condition by the express will of God, if its existence was inseparably connected with the greatest and most sacred

* Genises xlvi 13.

interests, with the religious destiny of the whole world,—can we be surprised that its law-giver imposed on it the rules indispensable to a wise policy, and brought universal charity under the restrictions necessary for the preservation of the nation? And, I dare affirm, that without such measures no earthly power could have saved the people of Israel from speedy destruction.

Christianity itself, has felt this full well. It quickly perceived that, in the Ethics it preached to the world, there was no place for the different nationalities,—these large individualities in the still larger family of man. Accordingly from the outset, with one hand it presents the Jews with their new code of morals, with the other it points to that Temple —which God and the people, religion and the state had made their most august abode—not a memorial stone of which the flames had allowed to remain. Accordingly, beside its ascetic morality it places its ascetic kingdom, its all-spiritual-Messiah, if I may use the expression; and in place of a political liberty it offers its votaries a spiritual one. Strangers to the struggle, the efforts, the sacrifices with which that heroic little band of Jews met the Romans in the last crisis of their national life, the Christians at Pella saw in the fall of Jerusalem and the Temple, the end of the earthly reign of that *law* whose spiritual overthrow they sought,—and the exile of a great nation was the first homage paid to the morality of the Gospels.

But a greater field opened before Christianity; its acts, influence and ethics were now to operate upon countless numbers, upon an empire a thousand times greater than Palestine. We take good care neither to overlook the benefits that this morality heaped upon the wretched of every kind, the comfort and new life that it brought them, nor to re-echo those old Pagan accusations that some modern authors have revived for their own benefit, wherein Christians were looked upon as conspirators, rebels and enemies of the Roman Empire. We shall only examine its relation to the patriotic sentiment, to religion, to love, and to a national existence. Now I say, that neither during the Roman nor any subsequent period had Christianity anything to present to feelings so natural to man; that it only impeded the natural development of these feelings, and that its action was always wavering, always hampered whenever it had to declare itself respecting patriotic duties. Christianity preached a great principle, *universal fraternity,*—a principle taken indeed from Judaism, but one in no wise tempered, as in the latter system, by *national fraternity.* On the contrary,

Christianity made, for the benefit of humanitarian brotherhood, that sacrifice, which the ancient legislators had made, sometimes of the individual to the family, by exagerating parental rights, and at others, of the family to the state, by the creation of this last absorbing personality. Christianity, then, skipped a step, and in its turn swept away nationalities from the affection of mankind. Impossible, thenceforth, to regard the political enemy other than a brother; impossible for the heart, the arm, not to tremble, whenever man, wounded man, or brethren smote each other, all men being according to Christianity, equal—that is, in the words of Paul himself, the Barbarian, Scythian, Greek and Jew. Can we in short, express this great truth more eloquently or boldly than an eminent writer has lately done: "*Patriotism*," says he, "*exists under the old law, but theoretically has no place in the new; and the day the Gospel was preached to the Gentiles was in tendency* THE LAST DAY OF NATIONALITIES." And again: "*The feeling of nationality, such as swells in the English breast, is an affection essentially Jewish. One might suppose that English society was a convention of the* CIRCUMCISED."

It must be said, however, that this equality was successively understood by Christianity in two different ways. At first it was only apathetic and indifferent as to national distinctions, and its Catholicism in this respect was but negative. But it soon changed its spirit; for, becoming triumphant, it sought to realize this equality, this universal brotherhood in a very tangible manner; and lo! the *Papacy* rose. And so we have, in one way or the other, the destruction of national diversities always arising from an *universal apathy* or an *universal empire*. And why? Because Christianity absolutely lacks a side, the social or political side,—either through the extravagance and exclusiveness of its ethics, or through its ultramundane aspirations, ever on the point of realization;—because with its ethics it had no jurisprudence, with an altar no throne, which in truth it merged in the former.

We are now about to glance at one of the main dangers, at one of the weakest spots in the Christian ethics; we are about to see that not only would it be very unjust (as we have shown) to compare a moral system on one side, with a political one on the other—that not only has Christianity this gap, this void which has made its existence embarrassed and embarrassing in the world—but that its beautiful morality, exquisite as it appears, could not, from its very refinement, evade the consequences of this blank, this want of the political element, which constitutes the weakness at once and the glory of Judaism; and that the great principle of *charity* destroyed itself, not being allowed to play its legitimate part with its kindred *justice*.

In vain did the new religion know only the spirit; in vain did it trample under foot, all the interests, all the wants of life; in vain did it incessantly fix its gaze upon the Kingdom of God, where it was to reign supreme; in vain did it predict the near advent of this, and plume itself as almost on the verge of the general resurrection, of a universal regeneration,—it could not, withal change the nature of things. The world kept on its way, in spite of all predictions to the contrary, and Christianity found itself involved in that world whose destruction it thought at hand, in that society whose transformation into immortal beings it had hoped soon to see, in those interests for which it had neglected to provide, in those rights and duties that political and social life begets. Persecuted at first, Christianity requited itself for the blood it generously shed—mingled nevertheless with that of the Jews—in all parts of the Empire. But its triumph prepared for it a much severer trial. Once master of that people upon which it had not reckoned, it would have escaped all danger, if it had like Judaism a king to place on the throne, a code to give the courts of justice, a policy with which to guide the chariot of State, and if it had taken care, like Judaism, to distinguish worldly, social and political concerns, from those relating to morals, religion and dogmas. But Christianity had only, and was only, a religion; *its law*, its state policy, its throne, were respectively, the dogma, the worship of God, and the altar. Master one time, of the world, whom shall it place upon the empty throne? Who is to hold the sword of the law? This is the crisis in the history of Christianity. Christianity, with the best intentions in the world, believed it could do nothing better than occupy the throne itself, than seize, itself, the scepter of justice, that is to say, subject to its dogmas, its religion and its laws, the public authority; in other words to enlist *law*, state, royalty in the service of its religion, to place its dogmas on an equal footing with political institutions, to substitute religion for national duties, and to give ethics the same rank as public virtues; in a word, to substitute for the citizen, conscience. Is this not what is called, in general terms, a state-religion? Now, what is a state-religion? It is conscience treated as a citizen, the mind subjugated, disciplined like the body, one's creed encompassed with penalties, executioners, pyres; it is violence, injustice, tyranny serving a religion all charity. And just because it had only charity, but no idea to justice, because it advocated only *love*, and not *respect*, because if devoted itself to the worship of virtues the most sublime, while it neglected those inferior perhaps, but equally holy and far more useful,—in fine because it aimed at being *more than just*, it was doomed to be *violent*.

And Judaism? It had a political system; it did not disdain to mix in the affairs of this world; it offered to the million, daily bread, air, sunlight, protection, good laws, justice to respect, a country to love, interests to care for, public virtues to practice, which, though not absolutely spiritual, were far more necessary—were (I may affirm) heaven brought to earth, because they are eternal truth—eternal beauty and eternal love ever applied to and intermingled with the concerns of life, *the Glory* (*Schechina*) which spans the earth. And—what is a thousand times more admirable and the proof of its divine origin—at the core of this Judaism, so homogeneous and compact, is ever a broad line of demarcation between religion and the state, the citizen and the monotheist, belief and justice, dogmas and the Law! In it, conscience, the sphere of faith, and the forum, the sphere of politics, never exchanged parts or powers. Never was remorse-supplanted by the scaffold, or hell by death. No-civil penalty for impiety, and no spiritual burden for the citizen. It had a code, solely politic, the *law of Moses;* and a code, solely religious, *tradition*. Not that the first has not the same origin and design as the second; not that the latter does not presuppose and supplement the former; but the one is rather the guide for the body, and prefers to speak to the citizen, to the people, to their interests, their remembrances, their hopes; the other is the guide rather of morals and of mind, and appeals more willingly to the conscience and the soul, to their past, their future, their eternal interests. To compare Christian ethics with the first is not only an injustice but an impropriety; for it exposes the nakedness of Christianity — exposes that void which has led charity to be less than just, in not reserving a suitable place for the duties and concerns of life.

But we must compare the ethics of Christianity with the simple unmixed ethics of Judaism. The former, as it is already suspected has doubtless its source chiefly in the sacred writings, but above all in tradition; it is this last principally that we are about to confront with the ethics of the Gospel. We shall not then be accused of choosing a ground favorable for the victory of Jewish ethics, so much and so long decried. The Pharisees have been so great a butt for the derision of the Church, and the latter seemed to stand in so little fear of a competition with them, that we hope these same poor Pharisees will be allowed to place before the judgment-seat of the nineteenth century the articles of their indictment, and the grounds of their secular condemnation. Besides, it is Judaism as it is that we contrast with Christian ethics. And far from imitating those who, fearing a flood, take refuge in the mountains, we shall not shield ourselves behind the Bible, (an object of veneration to both), to resist the pretensions of the Christian ethics. We shall take the *rabbinical*, traditional Judaism that centuries have made, and we think besides that we shall better serve the cause of criticism by thus studying Christianity in all its birth-surroundings, in the teachings and moral philosophy of that time, than by restricting ourselves to an antiquity, whose workings, though unquestionable, could not have been as precise, as evident or as consecutive, as those of Pharisaical Judaism.

CHAPTER II.

THE DOCTRINES UPON WHICH THE CHRISTIAN CODE OF MORALS IS FOUNDED—ABOLITION OF THE LAW—HOW IT IS UNDERSTOOD BY JESUS—FAITH WITHOUT WORKS—RUPTURE BETWEEN CATHOLICISM AND PROTESTANTISM—WITH PAUL, FAITH, WITHOUT WORKS, SAVES—CONTEMPT FOR THE BODY; MYSTICISM—IT ENDS IN IMMORALITY AND MATERIALISM; PROOFS FROM REASON AND HISTORY—GNOSTICISM AND ITS EXCESSES; ITS SEED IN THE GOSPEL.—THE SPIRITUALISM OF PAUL, WHAT—THE LIBERTY OF SPIRITUAL DEATH—THE FAITHFUL, DEAD IN JESUS CHRIST; ORIGIN OF THIS FICTION—THEY RISE WITH HIM; ANOTHER FICTION, ITS ORIGIN AND EFFECTS UPON MORALITY—THE REDEMPTION—"THE LAW, THE CAUSE OF SIN"— THE REDEMPTION OF THE JEW, THE CHRISTIAN.

But before proceeding with this comparison, let us examine whether certain doctrines, forming the basis of Christian ethics, are as sure and immoveable as represented. All agree, that a building, however large and splendid, affords no secure protection, if its solidity be not in proportion to its size. Are the foundations of the Christian ethics, so solid, that unaided, it irrisistably conquers all hearts?

An announcement made almost at the birth of Christianity, was calculated to have great influence in moulding the destiny of its ethics, and that was *the abolition of the Law.* Our duty at present is not to examine the great question concerning the relations of Jesus to the Law, or to what degree he advocated its preservation or annulment. If we might anticipate what we have to say respecting the Law, we should say that Jesus, thinking the era of the Messiah identical with that of the resurrection or universal regeneration, believed he was on the eve of legitimately abrogating **the Law**, when the dead, just before rising from their **graves, should** assume immortal bodies.

We shall soon have occasion to see what deep roots **this** belief **had in** existing Judaism, and how, for want of the reality, of **a proper and** real resurrection the Christians substituted **a** figurative one—a pure fiction. However that may be, *the abolition of the Law* was early proclaimed by Christianity. Now, it is easy to imagine into what trouble and confusion this bold stroke would throw the conscience, and what grand dangers a system of ethics, formulized, sanctioned and taught **by** this very Law whose fall it announced, was about to encounter. We ought to be able to cite facts and illustrations as to **the** results we indicate, and we shall accordingly **soon see** them teeming, after we shall have enumerated the **causes which** left Christianity, from its very origin, **at** the **mercy of the waves of** opinion, and even exposed to destruction. **What we wish to state here** is the fatal precedent **that** Christianity **established against morality** by this abolition **of the Law.** For mark well: when a nation possesses a **revealed code, meant to** rule the mind, when **in this** revelation the entire **life** of a **people is** regulated and **marked out in** advance, **when** neither **the** actions, the feelings nor the moral relations of man with man escape its provisions, when finally the **ethical** system, of the same parent as the jurisprudence, the political economy, the mode of worship, the religious doctrines, —shakes off its authority; when this nation, accustomed for ages to regard this revelation as its rule of conduct in ethics as well as religion, and the most natural ethical precepts as positive laws, is told some fine day that this law "is played out," that it was only the type and shadow of what was to come, that, at best, it was only good for children, that it is the source of *"death and sin,"* nothing better than *"wretched slavery"* (Paul), that a law of freedom (?) is about to replace it; when this great word, *freedom,* is sounded in a thousand ways and on all occasions; much more, when the Gentiles, who know nothing of the law of Moses, **hear that** a revelation which had provided for ethics as well as worship, is about to give way to a law of grace, of freedom—who does not see that morality is struck down with doctrine, worship and legislation? Where shall reason take refuge when this great catastrophe arrives? For let it be well understood, here is not a reason of philosophy which, by its own strength, has formed a system of ethics purely rational; nor yet a dawning reason, that distinguishes what comes from its own nature from within, from what comes to it from without—but the reason of antiquity, of all time, of every kind, that admits and recognizes a revelation. What shall it substitute for this ruined ethical system? It has neither an ethics of philosophy nor of nature to put in its place; it has only *sentiment*, and of that it avails itself. This, in my opinion, is the most probable explanation of that predominance of sentiment in the Christian ethics. This is why its first founders incessantly appeal to sentiment and not to reason; this is the source from which the Christian ethics has drawn the grace, pathos and delicacy that so characterize it; and hence, too, the horror of polemical disputation, *Faith* usurping the place of *logic and science*.

In vain, truly, would it have appealed to reason, for this would have always opposed to its new masters, that law of Moses, that Judaism, ethical no less than doctrinal and legislative, given by the very God that was preached yet repudiated. In vain would it have added that the will of God, changed as to all else, had remained fixed and unaltered as to ethics; in vain would it have laboriously gleaned and sifted from civil and religious ordinances, from doctrine and ritual, those moral precepts blended and incorporated with the general system, to construct something independent, sacred and inviolable from the wreck of Judaism. Reason would have rejected these arbitrary distinctions. It would have pointed to the same God, the same revelation giving the most sublime moral precepts, as, *To love one's neighbor as one's self*, in conjunction with the humblest, the most mysterious of ritual prohibitions against the *mixing of seeds*. It would have said that if the will of God changed on one point it might change on another; that no difference of language, no mark, in this system so homogeneous, indicated what was for a time, and what was for ever; that the ceremonials of the system, its rewards, punishments, and exhortations gave the ethical part no special, independent or privileged place; that quite the contrary, penalties the most terrible, rewards the most munificent were attached to the ceremonial laws, exactly, perhaps, because they have such weak roots in the heart and reason of man. Such is the language of reason. And this language was, in all probability actually uttered, not only by the faithful, but forced likewise, by logic and good sense, from the apostles themselves, and above-all from those who took the most active part in the abolition of the Law. Among the latter the chief place certainly belongs to Paul. Now what is the new principle proclaimed by him? It is faith; faith as the highest virtue enjoined on mankind, faith opposed as such not only to science, to vain disputes, to vain jargon, as we have elsewhere observed, but also faith opposed as such to *works;* that is to say,—if one believes in Jesus, the God—Messiah, in his personal divinity and mission, in the efficacy of his death, in his resurrection, he has no longer need of works to obtain salvation.

We should be sorely grieved, could it be thought **for an instant** that we wished to calumniate the Christian ethics. **No one** disputes the truth of what we are about to say. Christians **of every** sect and color agree, that Paul, the great Christian legis**lator** and moralist, teaches the doctrine of justification by faith without works. But the principle thus laid down appeared so revolting, so opposed to the noblest instincts of the human heart, so contrary to the sentimental morality Christianity was preaching, that restrictions were soon made to narrow its scope. While Protestantism, obeying logic and reason alone, drew boldly from this principle all its consequences and proclaimed moral works *useless* and *pernicious*, faith alone being sufficient for salvation; Catholicism, on the other hand, having an external authority, social and political, being itself at once a government and a religion, recoiled in terror, from these destructive consequences, from this licentious morality, and interpreted the "works" of Paul in the most restricted sense, namely as the *works of the Law*, as the practice of the Mosaical code, and declared, against the Protestants in the council of Trent, the necessity of good **works.** It was a return to the old Hebrew ethics, it was a total rejection of the Apostle of the Gentiles, it was a great diminution of the importance, the efficacy of the redemption.

Accordingly, we see the Protestants use towards the Catholics the same language Paul used towards the Pharisees and Judaizing Christians, and class the Catholics with the Jews. "*The Catholic doctors*, says Mosheim, "*confound the Law with the Gospel, and represent everlasting happiness as the reward of good works.* **Is** it not here lies the true sense, the veritable intention of Paul?" This is the ground upon which, as we have just said, the great battle between Protestants and Catholics took place. The ethics of Paul is, in our opinion, that indeed which reason and independent criticism gave him through the mouth of Protestantism. The arguments and verbiage of Paul are express thereon. He presents us, as an example of his theory, *Abraham* justified not by works but by faith.[*] Now, the works of Abraham, which "were not reckoned to him for righteousness," according to Paul, were not, as far as I know, *works of* the Law, which had not as yet been given, but truly moral works, in the strictest sense; charity, justice, hospitality, philanthropy, teaching,

---

[*] Rom. iv. 1, 2, 3, 4.

virtue, monotheism sown among the Gentiles. And, nevertheless, Abraham was not justified by his works, but indeed by his faith. Could any one, who referred only to the works of the Law, so speak? And, furthermore, I affirm, that if the example chosen by Paul be altogether conclusive, the language used and the consequences drawn are altogether unmistakeable: *"For what saith the Scripture? Abraham believed God, and it was counted unto him for righteousness. Now to him that worketh is the reward not reckoned of grace, but of debt."** Here, then, we have all title to recompense, all meritorious works declared null. This is not all: "But to him that worketh not, but believeth on him that justifieth the ungodly, his faith is counted for righteousness."† Thus, no doubt is possible—without works, and however *wicked*, one's faith alone in him who justifies the wicked, saves. Do we want more? Hear Paul, in continuation: " *Even as David also describeth the blessedness of the man unto whom God imputed* RIGHTEOUSNESS WIHOUT WORKS, *saying: 'Blessed are they whose iniquities are forgiven and whose sins are covered. He to whom the Lord will not impute sin.'*" That is to say, according to the sense given by Paul to these words of David, the grace of faith confers remission of sin, the imputation of righteousness. And in Romans (iii. 27), "boasting" is declared "excluded," not by the "law of works," but by the "law of faith." And so in the Epistle to the Galatians (ii. 16), he teaches that man is not justified by the *works of the Law* (without any distinction), but solely by faith in Jesus Christ. It is true that in the third Epistle to the Romans, verse 31, the Apostle declares that he does not wish to *"make void the law by faith,"* but on the contrary, to *"establish" it;* and that in the Epistle to the Galatians (ii. 17) he exhorts *against sinning*, but, in the first place, that was because he imitated in this respect the language of the Master, who saw in Christianity only whatever was spiritual and permanent, real and tangible in the old law itself; and in the second, because he himself felt all the danger of his principles, foresaw the immorality that might arise in the world under the shield of faith alone justifying. In fine, I affirm, that if he condemns sin, if he does not want all the license consistent with faith, it is for the sake of expediency, and for a purely secondary consideration. For, mark well, it is not in the name of truth, justice or virtue, absolutely, that Paul permits not sin under the rule of faith, but it is because faith, fully equal to the pardon of every crime, could *not very well* be made the accomplice and instrument of evil, nor "Christ the

* Rom vi. 5.   † Rom. iv. 3-4.

minister of sin." **See to what a point** Christianity must descend to find a prop for **its ethics, after** having taken away its old and natural base, **the Law !**

Would we **glance at** the necessary and natural links that, in **the minds of** Christians, united good works with the law-making **both solid** and inseparable. They are that Paul, who wants faith **without** works, is the greatest enemy to the ceremonial law ; **and that, on** the other hand, James, perhaps the most **conservative apostle** and the advocate of the necessity of works, is also **the most** favorable to the law.

This is not the only peril that Christianity made its ethics incur. Is there no danger in **this** contempt for the body, for "this sinful flesh that hampers us, and that we should detest," and in Christianity's launching its anathemas against matter, and making this the object of its rabid tirades? Are self-denial, martyrdom, heroism, **the only results ? We** admit, willingly, that contempt of the **body,** when **made a** rule of life, begets often marvellous virtues, which the world admires, and that it **proved a powerful** support against the rude shocks Christianity at first **encountered.** But besides the world, there is a power called logic, which, sooner or later, draws from every principle all the conclusions it involves. Now, it can be fearlessly asserted, that from contempt of the body, of the flesh, as it was understood **and** practised by Christianity, must one day come the vilest **materialism,** the most unbridled licentiousness, the most shock**ing** immorality. Doubtless, there appears to be nothing so paradoxical, so incredible as the union of contempt for the body with sensuality. **But logic** and history prove that this is not only possible but almost always inevitable. **What does** logic teach? That one may be a materialist and addicted to all carnal excesses in two different ways. Matter may be paid an extravagant worship, be thought alone worthy of our care and love, **be** considered as the whole of man, over whom it should hold despotic sway, and that no rein or restriction should be put on its **demands.** But the materialism of which we speak is of another kind ; **it is** when a super-refinement of spiritualism cuts assunder the constituent parts of our being, and by care and effort detaches the spirit from its earthly shrine ; when, by dint of **zeal, self**denial and indefatigable perseverance it succeeds in isolating the noblest part of our nature, in snapping all the links that bind it to the body, and in giving it an existence absolutely independent of the necessities and reactions of the flesh ; when through this gulf of separation it succeeds in attaining this vaunted apostolic *liberty*, wherein the spirit, no longer bound to earth, soars to a sphere where the echo of life's joys and woes do not come. A great proof, doubtless, of the nobleness of our nature, but likewise a perilous flight, a fatal separation! since the seductive liberty gained for the spirit sets free also all the vilest instincts of the animal. No more influence now, it is true, of the body upon the spirit, but also no more control of the body by the soul. Why should it descend to concern itself about a miserable animal? Why should it dwell with a thing so full of care, turmoil and disorder, to be its governor and guide? This is how an excessive contempt for the flesh ends in materialism, as we have just seen that the vilest materialism springs from too great an esteem and consideration for the flesh. This is the teaching of logic. Does experience speak less loudly? Does not history show us that whenever mysticism allows itself full rein, it is inevitably dragged into the most monstrous excesses, the most ignoble pleasures, sometimes by the impetuosity of a body abandoned to itself, and, what is not a little singular, at others, by a sensuality regulated, established, sanctioned in advance by that very spiritualism which, a little while ago, disdained to enjoin on the body order, temperance, virtue, duty?

Far from us the thought of renewing against Christianity the old pagan accusations! Far from us the thought of charging to the evangelical Christians those banquets, festivals and orgies that scandalized the decent folks of Paganism! We far prefer to say, with the Christian apologist, that it was the Gnostics solely who astonished and shocked the world by these hideous exhibitions. Still the Gnostics were Christians, wicked ones, if you will, disorderly and sensual, but accepting the dogmas, principles and preaching of Christianity, though attaching themselves chiefly to Peter and Paul, as we shall show elsewhere; and, above all, the causes and seeds of these strange abuses lay truly in the Gospels. Do they not announce in every page the contempt and condemnation of the flesh? Do they not declare its works null, useless for salvation, provided there be faith in Jesus Christ? Do they not advocate a worship *in spirit* as the highest degree of human perfection? Do they not propose to man, as his noblest task here below, the detachment of his spirit from the flesh of sin, so as to gain this "*liberty of the children of God*," procured by faith, and not by works, the evidence, per contra, of lapse and slavery? And, to connect this ethical system with its speculative side, do they not sacrifice and fuse matter, *the inferior mother*, to the weal of mind, of the world to come, of idealism, of *the superior mother*. Do they not term true Christians *the spiritual?* Now, if we wish to know exactly what is the *spiritual* of the apostle we have but to view the neoplatonism of Plotinus, Porphery and Proclus, the Gnostic system, and, above both, the corresponding distinctions of the Cabala. What do the first two establish on this score? They divide, as we know, men into three classes: the *Hyloists*, (the lowest rank) that is to say, the "carnal" of Paul, who were, according to the Gnostics, the Pagans; the *Psychics*, or Animists, and these were, according to the same, the Jews and the non-Gnostic Christians; last, the Pneumatics, the spiritual, and they were exclusively the Gnostics. Now we know what was the "Pneumatic" of the Gnostics: man, above law, usages, virtue, for whom all is good, all allowable, since his soul, in spite of any liberty the body may assume, can contract, henceforth, no stain, having an existence quite apart from the flesh that surrounds it. We do not quite assert that the spiritualism of Paul was of this kind; or that the contempt of the body and of its works was pushed by him to this point; but if he be not the type and model of the system he is, beyond question, its prime cause, and the Pneumatic of Gnosticism is, at the very least, a Paulite in excess.

We have tried to fix the meaning of Paul's "spiritual" through its reflection in the "Pneumatic" of the Gnostics. We may, with advantage, as a counter-test, compare both with their type, *Cabalistic spiritualism*. We may boldly affirm that the tripple distinction of the Gnostics, and the spiritual of Paul become quite intelligible only by linking them with the equivalent Cabalistical doctrine. The Cabalists say that man has a threefold nature; the breath, (NEFESCH) which has its root in the emanation, *Malkhout* (called also Nefesch); the ROUACH or soul, that is connected with the *logos*, with the *tiphereth* that bears its name; lastly, the NESCHAMA, that has its source in the *Bina*, in the Holy Spirit, superior, like that which is in man. This is not all; the same classification of men by their predominant nature is made by the Cabalists as by the Gnostics. With those, as with these, the great mass of the faithful attain only to *nefesch*, to *Malkhout*, to the *hylism* of the Neoplatonists and the Gnostics, to the *flesh* of Paul; their portion is the *letter*, the bondage of the letter, as Paul says the literal sense (peschat) of the Law, and they bear, like Paul's charnels, the name *slaves*, for the malkout itself is called slave, or else they are given the title of *eggs* not yet laid (betsim). In this system, as in the other, we see those to whom the *Rouach* has been allotted, who have their root in the Tiphereth, the Logos; that is to say the Psychists, the learned, the scribes, the doctors of Paul and the Gospels, who reach the legal, philosophical and theoretic sense of

the Law, and these are chickens scarcely hatched (efrochim).
Lastly, we arrive at the elect souls, supported by Neschama,
that is to say, the Pneumatics of the Gnostics and Plotinus, the
spiritual of Paul, who have their source and seat in Bina, (the
superior spirit) and to whom Cabalistic science (*sod*) unveils its
mysteries; these are the *free*, for Bina is called Freedom (*deror,
cherout*); and far from being slaves, eggs or chickens, they are
the legitimate *sons, children* entitled to the patrimony. See
how the rays, scattered everywhere through this work, converge
to this luminous point! The spirituality to which Christians
are invited is naturally linked to the Cabalistic model of the
Holy Spirit, the Bina; both make the same use of the study and
dissemination of the Cabalistic mysteries, that confer exactly
the title and rights of the spiritual (mare demischmeta). By the
same system, for raising themselves to the Bina, they acquired
the title *children*, which, as opposed to that of *slaves*, the
Cabala used long before Christainity. They acquired at the same
time the "*liberty*" proper to this degree, one of its most characteristic designations, which the Cabala never used in its practical
sense, (unless as regards a soul freed from the bonds of the body)
but which Christianity first, and then the Gnostics so strangely
abused. This last consideration leads us to speak of another
cause still that makes the foundation of the Christian ethics
weak and insecure, that opens the door to every abuse, and
though producing noble acts through the ascendancy of the soul
over the body, also gives the latter all the vices of an ignorant
and ungoverned slavery. What we are about to say is, at first
sight so improbable, that, had we not the proofs ready, we would
not dare state it. One of the doctrines of Rabbinical Judaism,
very natural, common enough and almost useless to teach, was
one referring to certain obituary customs. Already had the
Bible and the Hebrew prophets, highly prizing life, said in a
thousand places that the law, virtue, the commands of God,
cease at the door of the tomb; that the dead no more praise the
Lord; that the sepulchre gives forth no song of thanks; passages
which have been given in a materialistic sense, but which, for
orthodox Judaism, is quite another thing as we see. Pharisaism
formulizes them into one general saying, the terms of which are
of special importance in order to penetrate the true meaning of
many evangelical passages and especially from Paul. The Pharisees say: "*With the dead is liberty* (from the Psalms), *when one
is dead he is freed from precepts.*" It is almost incredible, but
this is the sole pivot upon which the words and thoughts of Paul
incessantly turn, in the thousand places where he speaks of the

liberty of the dead. Here **is** the origin, the cause of one of the boldest fictions that ever emanated from the human mind—a fiction, the consequences of which were incalculable. Paul wants the faithful to identify themselves with Christ, to believe that they are his very embodiment, and that their flesh is condemned, crucified and dead with him. By this death which they share with him they acquire the most precious freedom, viz., the freedom from the law. Can the law rule a dead body? Can it extend its sceptre beyond the tomb? Can it exact from a dead man the practice of its rites and ceremonies?

And, furthermore, to touch on another point, suggested by the words of Paul himself, what is the Cabalistic doctrine regarding original sin, spiritual new-birth? Is it not the *law* or *death* which it names as the sole means of making the ticcoun or reparation for the first sin? Well, of these two means, says Paul, we have chosen the last. We are dead—dead, indeed, with Jesus; *we are in him and he is in us; he has died for all; he has crucified in himself our flesh of sin; by dying on the cross he has fulfilled for us the whole Law.* Behold us, then, in full life, come into the precious liberty of pure souls, and no one can henceforth charge the dead with neglect of the Law. Have we transcended the thoughts and expressions of Paul himself? Then let us cite his words: "*Our flesh is considered as dead if Christ is in us.*" "*He who is dead is freed from sin.*" Rom. vi, 7. But what is much more important: "Know ye not, brethren, (for I speak to them who know the Law)—that is, to those who were not ignorant of the Pharisaical ideas as to the duration of its observance—know ye not that the Law hath dominion over a man as long as he liveth?" And having exemplified his position by saying that a woman is free to marry after her husband's death, he continues, (v. 4): "Wherefore, my brethren, ye also are become dead to the Law, by the body of Christ, that ye should be married to another, to him who is raised from the dead. For when WE WERE in the flesh, the motions of sins, which were by the Law, did work in our members. But now we are delivered from the Law, *being dead* (we follow in this place the true translation of Diodata) to that wherein we were held." Much more; the sin of Adam, the cause of the Law with the Cabalists and Paul, is expiated by the death of Jesus; he dies, is buried, and his disciples are likewise with him. Our flesh has been condemned to suffer for all in Jesus. There is then no more condemnation for those who are in Jesus, who walk not after the flesh but after the spirit. * * * For what was impossible to the Law (to give perfect liberty in atoning for even original sin) in that it was weak through the flesh, God, sending his own son in the likeness of sinful flesh, and for sin condemned sin in the flesh in order that the righteousness of the Law might be fulfilled in us. (Rom. viii, 1-4)

We shall not multiply citations. A simple reading of Paul's writings will show their spirit much better than detached fragments. What they clearly testify is the strange abuse that is made of a simple *fiction*, and the consequence drawn from it with incredible coolness, viz.: the abolition of the Law. But in this tomb of the Law—in this inaction of the dead, shall not morality itself be annihilated? Have we not to fear that *this defunct* will free himself from virtue, from moral obligations, as well as from ceremonial injunctions? And is there, moreover, no danger that those members, said to be dead, should refuse to perform the most holy duties, or that the spirit, having attained its natural freedom, should think itself no longer obliged to lay any restraint on the flesh which surrounds it, but which is already dead and crucified in Jesus?

But the fiction continues: These faithful, dead and buried with Jesus, rise with him; our flesh, too, is considered as risen with Jesus. We are dead to the Law that we may belong to another, viz., to him who is risen from the dead; and Jesus, our brother, is the first born from the dead. No doubt possible. For Jesus, and, after him, for his disciples, the era of the resurrection, the renewing of nature, the resurrection of bodies was about to commence; and for the successors of Jesus, it had already come in his own person, in his body gone living from the tomb and become the first-born of the dead. But what gives this fiction quite an exceptional importance is the sense it took from its contact with the doctrines of the day. What did the Pharisees understand by the resurrection? Beyond doubt it took in not only human bodies called to a new life, furnished with superior organs and powers, but also the whole of nature in a general renovation, in a new birth that was to change the aspect of nature; and it would be, doubtless, both a curious and instructive study to compare this doctrine with its ancient or modern imitations. The Pharisaic school, in accord on this point, differed as to the time of the general resurrection, and as to its connexion with the Messianic era. One party made these two eras absolutely contemporaneous, and not only was the Messiah to usher Israel into an era of prosperity, safety and liberty, but also to give the signal for the renovation and rebirth of nature, of which the most solemn and striking event would naturally be the resurrection of the dead. The other party viewed things in quite a different light. Placing the resurrectional era at the remotest possible period, **they** regarded the coming of the Messiah only as a simple social **change, wherein** the laws of nature would remain the same, **and things go on** as usual; or, to sum the whole with **an adage,** *Nothing be changed except slavery to liberty.* **We** need **not say to** which of these schools Christianity belonged. For it no interval, no possible distinction between the Messianical and the resurrectional era; and though the contrary doctrine conclusively prevailed in Judaism, the sychronism of the two eras alone found **favor** with Christianity.

From this first difference **arose** another. Although the Pharisees protracted as much as possible the reign of the Law, yet they made it **cease at** the threshold of the resurrection. As the material world was to undergo a complete change, so a new *law*, springing from new social conditions, was to supplant the old religion. On that new earth, in the midst of new beings and new conditions, **the** thought of God, the *law of God*, self-sufficing and naturally self-conserving, would change in its applications as it changes even here below, according to circumstances, to bodies, to relations, **as it is** applied to world, sun **or** star. **Here** is the origin **and true** sense **of** this mass of sentences, propositions, similitudes, in which the idea of a new law, a new covenant, and annulled prohibitions shines through images and allegories that **have been** so often used pervertedly against Jewish orthodoxy, and that Christian polemics has incessantly thrown **in** the face of the **rabbis.** These were the very ideas that prevailed among the Judao-Christians at the *abolition of the Law,* **just as in** general all that subsequently became a weapon in the hands of established Christianity, had been once an originating **power,** a cause in primitive Christianity. Nothing easier, nothing more inevitable after what we have said, than the abolition of the Law. The era of the Messiah being identified completely **in** the minds of **the** primitive Christians with that of the resurrection (this having **already** commenced with the resurrection of Jesus, the first-born **of the** dead), and the whole church, deeming the destruction and renovation of the world imminent, the first conclusion was that the **law of** Moses was about to be superseded by another law more in unison **with** the semi-spiritual state of **the new** society. In vain was **this** expectation disappointed from **day to day; in vain** did the resurrection proper keep ever retreating towards the future, and in vain were people already, as we learn from the Epistles, devoured by impatience. Never mind; its shade, its image, a resurrection quite fictitious can always be substituted for the real resurrection; it can be taught, that the faithful, dead with Jesus, are raised with him; that the **reign of** the resurrection, of the new birth commenced with the resurrection of Jesus, **and thus the abolition of the Law can always progress.**

We need not dwell at length on the peril in which ethics, religion and practical morality were placed by such a system. This equivocal position created by Christianity in the actual order of things; this society, which is no longer the human society that the actual laws would have, nor yet the society of the resurrection, such as it will be one day; this systematized contradiction between existence as it should be and existence as it was, between the resurrection as a hypothesis and life as a thesis; this fiction of daily and hourly recurrence—was it calculated to strengthen sceptical minds, wavering wills, or those of selfish passions, in the worship and love of the good? All relations about to cease, all ties to be broken, society to disappear, and this ephemeral life to have, perhaps, no morrow; all affections, wants, tears, rights, duties, the living, throbbing reality of life sacrificed to an abstraction, to a chimera, to a rabbinical subtlety of Saul's—is such a system calculated to win people inevitably to the performance of duty, to a respect for all rights, to a veneration for the affections? But these loves, rights, duties are *nothing now* in the rights acquired by the resurrection, nothing but an empty name, an appearance that shall soon dissolve to smoke. So that here, as elsewhere, morality shares the fate of the law; and, if new legal relations are about to be established in the new society—for, according to Jesus himself, in the new world are to be no more marriages—new moral relations must be thenceforth the guide of our conduct. But the abolition of the law, the death and resurrection of Jesus—the causes, as we have just seen, of doubt and weakness in the Christian ethics—themselves contain what compromises, no less seriously, morality. This is the Redemption. Now, the idea of a redemption lessens in many ways at once the value, beauty and grandeur of morality. What is the Redemption, and what does it suppose? It supposes *a state of innocence* anterior to sin, and wherein the redemption by the blood of the lamb can replace man; it supposes sin itself, and the expiatory sacrifice of the God-Messiah. Let us see the share, good or bad, that these three elements have in the formation of the Christian ethics. Is this restoration to a state of innocence, to Adam's state before sin, unattended by **danger?** Judaism also proposed to its adherents a means of regaining the privileges lost by the first transgression. It also had **an** Incarnate Word to work this miracle; but this word was the thought of God embodied in the Law, maintaining itself from age to age, reinstating man, his actions and his life, and through him the whole creation. But the last act of **this great drama,** the return **to** Adam's condition, to paradise, **took place at the** era of the **resurrection,** when men, improved by **the** regenerating works **of the Law, by** the trials of life, by **the slow and** progressive initiation **of** actual existence, should **assume** bodies like Adam's before **his sin.** Until then the **regeneration** is not complete, sin has **not** abandoned **his** prey; **the chain** by which it holds us falls off indeed, link by **link, but the** last link is broken only by the tomb. Must Christianity **wait so** long? No; doubtless, for to it the door of the resurrection **lies** already open; this state we have reached; **in** this we **live,** if **it be** true that the resurrection of Jesus and **of the just** at the time **of** his death, are the **first** fruits of **the** general resurrection, and **he** the first born of the dead. Innocent as **Adam,** ignorant as **he,** because the fatal fruit is considered as **never** having been eaten, subjected **not to the real laws** that rule the present physical world, but to those **of the sinless world, to** those that shall rule it after the resurrection, **to** fictitious **laws, to an** imaginary world, to this resurrection **that** ought to be inaugurated by Jesus, **how** should we be **less** free, less capable of sin **and** evil than **Adam** himself, had he **never** tasted **the** forbidden fruit?

We understand very well the difficulty **that a modern will have** in admitting these conclusions. We admit that **the** religious **instinct,** the pure morals, the sacred traditions which Christianity **drew from the** Synagogue, fought effectually against the power of **logic,** against the enticement to the licentiousness which these **doctrines** authorized. But radical vice is **no less** visible in the principles; **and** their fruits—bitter enough—soon showed themselves in those Adamites **of** the first and twelfth centuries, in the Turlupines of the fourteenth, **in the Picards** of the fifteenth century;—all of whom took **their starting-point** from the principles which we denounce.

Let us now see **the effects of original** sin (as understood **by** Christianity), especially **in its relations** to the Law. **We can scarce** credit our senses, as **we** see **the** great difficulties **of his position,** the contest with orthodox Judaism, the hatred and sworn **destruction to** the law of **Moses,** drive Paul **to** those straits in which **morality,** that plank of the wreck he wished to save, **m**ust be lost. **Paul** has a theory which Georgias, Hobbes, or the deceased Proudhon, the inventor of anarchy, would **not** have disowned, and **w**hich, once admitted, would be the *coup de grace* to all justice, **all** law, all morality, all society—namely, that not only is the Law **a** result of **the** first sin, **but** that it *constitutes and is the cause of our sins*—that without the Law there is no sin, and that consequently you have but to suppress the Law to make sin disappear. Nothing can be more exact than the statement: *It is through the Law that we know sin.** The Law worketh wrath; for where there is no Law there is no transgression.† *By one man sin entered into the world* (speaking to those who wished to limit the sense of the word *sin* to transgressions against the Mosaic Law); for, until the Law, sin was in the word; but sin is not imputed where there is no law.‡ And further on: "For as by one man's disobedience many were made sinners (probably in allsorts of sin) so by the obedience of one shall many be made *righteous*" (probably, also, in all sorts of righteousness, moral and Mosaic). *Moreover, the Law entered, that offense might abound.*§ This is enough, but it is not all: *When we were in the flesh* (we are at present in spiritual life, under the law of the *spirit* and not of the letter), *the motions of sins, which were by the Law* (meaning sinful affections) *did work in our members to bring forth fruit unto death.* "*But now we are delivered from the Law, being dead to that wherein we were held; that we should serve in newness of spirit, and not in the oldness of the letter.*" ‖ Can we still doubt that the moral laws as well as the ceremonial were included in these singular theories? Let us say so if we can? The Law is not given for the just, but for sinners, and for those who cannot be classified, for people without religion, 1st and 2d commandment; for the profane, 3d commandment; for murderers of parents, 5th commandment; for homicides, 6th commandment; for fornicators, 7th commandment; for men-stealers, 8th commandment, (as understood by the Pharisees, showing what studies and influences inspired the apostle); for liars, 9th commandment; and for perjurers, 10th commandment. But this is nothing to what follows: "What shall we say then? Is the Law sin? God forbid. Nay, I HAD NOT KNOWN SIN BUT BY THE LAW; for I had not known lust, except the Law had said: 'Thou shalt not covet.' But sin, taking occasion by the commandment, wrought in me all manner of concupiscence. For without the Law sin was dead. For I was once alive without the Law, but when the commandment came sin revived, and I died."¶ Do we wish language still more exact and serious? "The sting of death is sin, and the strength of sin is the Law."** Much more; the ministration of the Law is a ministration of condemnation.†† And as the corollary to all these axioms: "There is therefore no longer any condemnation for those who are in Christ-Jesus, who walk not after the flesh but after the spirit." See what is asserted.

* Rom. iii. 20. † iv. 15. ‡ v. 12–13.
, v. 19 20. ‖ vii. 5–6. ¶ Rom. vii. 7–9.
** 1 Cor. xv. 56. †† 11 Cor. iii. 9.

The only sign by which we recognize *sin* is by the prohibition, and the sole distinctive characteristic of evil is its condemnation. It is the Law that originates at its pleasure good or evil, and we have but to change, to abolish the Law that all sin may likewise disappear.

Nevertheless, certain as we are that such is the meaning of Paul's language, and that these principles lead directly to the subversion of the simplest principles of right and wrong, we must not withhold our conviction that Paul's brain and heart revolted against the possible deductions; and one of the best proofs of our correctness is to see Paul himself guarding against the possible application of his teachings, so apt to let loose upon the world the most dreadful vices and abuses. "What, then?" he cries, "shall we sin because we are not under the Law, but under grace?"* This was the time to escape at once, or never, from this fatal consequence, by loudly proclaiming that distinction which some theologians have infelicitously established in the Law itself, between the ceremonial laws which Paul wished to abolish, and the moral laws which he wished to preserve.

Why then did he, too, not use it? Why, if he admitted it, did he not seize upon this distinction so simple, natural and convenient to free himself from the difficulty? Paul, however, does not seem even to dream of this. He prefers to entangle himself in a labyrinth of—we shall not say sophisms—but dialectical subtleties and syllogisms, quite Talmudical, difficult to follow, of which the most probable conclusion, arrived at with slow, uncertain and embarrassed steps, is this: That *the new state being a servitude to Justice or to God, instead of the old one which was a servitude to sin, the deliverance from the latter does not dispense us from paying due homage to the former, that is, from conforming to the divine will, by which alone we are freed from the yoke of the Law.* Here is a rather obscure word-battle; but it is not our fault, nor even Paul's; it is, on the contrary, to his credit, for by it alone can he escape the frightful consequences which his principles, rigorously used, could not fail to bear.

In short, if the innocence and sin which the redemption supposes are little favorable to Christian ethics, shall the redemption itself be more so,—the redemption or the *sacrifice of a God-man*, this remedy applied to the old sore of humanity?

Judaism, too, as we have said, recognizes a Word (Tipheret, Logos); it styles it, additionally, the Law, Torah; it believes in its incarnation in the *Malkhout*, the *Torah schebealpe, tradition;* and the office of this Word or Torah, descended to us, the guide of our thoughts and actions, is to efface gradually the marks of

* Rom. vi. 15.

the old slavery, to atone for the sin of the first man. But how does the redemption work in Judaism? By making of man himself, of his conscience, soul, and will, the first, chief, and—I had almost said—the only means of his renovation, in summoning him to open his mind and heart to the teachings, exhortations, light and warmth emanating from the divine word, so that the whole inner man be transformed, his strength aroused, his powers expanded, and he himself alone brought to work, under the eye and hand of God, for his own salvation. In short, the redemption of Judaism is altogether from within, because its Word is so too, because its dogma, ethics and worship have no reality or sphere here below, except so far as man seizes, assimilates and realizes in himself the perfections they contain. Without this assimilation of the Divine Word, this all-penetrating bread, this perpetual SUPPER where the incarnate Word for ever supplies the table of Judaism, what would be this Word itself? Nothing but a guest, a divine one indeed, but one which thro' lack of entertainment could not bring to our spiritual hearths those treasures of blessing with which it is laden. One cannot, then, but perceive how eminently favorable are Jewish doctrine, its incarnate Word and Redemption to man's dignity which they raise, to his moral energy which they arouse, to his interior transformation—alone reliable, because it is his own work—to his true justification, the fruit of a slow, inward labor, that leaves no dark corner of the mind or conscience unpenetrated by the divine light! Is it thus with Christianity? Its Word, its Redemption, its action upon the human soul, are, undeniably, all exterior, all objective; they operate outside of man, without his taking any part whatever, except an act of faith in the virtue and efficacy of Jesus' sacrifice, according to some, or at most (according to others) an act of general faith in Jesus, his mission, commands, and promises. The merits that justify, that procure pardon, are ever those of another, namely, of Jesus. Never does man himself conquer them by the sweat of his brow; they are *imputed* to him. Ever will remain this vast difference between Christianity and Judaism, viz: that the Redemption of the latter is altogether interior; that its Passion, Condemnation, Death, Garden of Olives, Prætor and Golgotha, are internal facts, the sphere of all being the mind and heart of man, where the Word is ceaselessly sacrificed for the benefit of humanity, upon the altar that man erects.

The foundations, then, as we see, upon which Christianity rests, far from having that solidity which the beauty of the structure seems to promise, are, on the contrary, fraught with dangers, that a rigid logic could not fail to show.

CHAPTER III.

HISTORICAL RESULTS.

SCANDALS IN THE CHURCH—EMBARRASSMENT OF THE APOSTLES—THE NICOLAITES—THE PROPHETESS OF THYATIRA—THE SIMONIANS—OTHER GNOSTIC SECTS—SECTS OF THE MIDDLE AGES—PRINCIPLES OF GNOSTIC IMMORALITY; INFERENTIAL THEORY—JUDAISM KNOWS NOTHING SIMILAR—SOLITARY EXCEPTION CONFIRMATORY OF OUR SYSTEM—PROTESTANTISM AND ITS ETHICAL SYSTEMS—QUIETISM.

We have hitherto studied but the speculative side of Christian ethics, its roots in dogma, and the influence that the latter can and must exert upon morals. We have strictly confined ourselves to the circle of ideas, avoiding all proof *a posteriori*, only that we may proceed orderly in our exposition. In confining ourselves to the region of abstractions, perhaps we may have appeared desirous of avoiding realities that could falsify our conclusions, and of giving ourselves free rein in endless reasoning, without ever appealing to the test of experience. But this would be a great mistake. Far from avoiding reality and experience, or rejecting all proof *a posteriori*, we have deferred them only to give them a larger and **more** suitable place. The principles already mentioned, the defects already discovered, the germs of weakness, degeneracy and corruption, we are about to see in the external **world,** exerting their influence, developing their inherent baneful powers, and spreading their deadly branches and leaves over a **section of** mankind. We are about to view hideous displays, to see repulsive theories, distorted doctrines and unparalleled views, shelter themselves under the principles of Christianity, and cover its trunk with a rank vegetation,—quickly lopped down, it is true, by the authority of the Church, but which does not fail to prove, on the one hand, that we were right in our perception of this fatal germ in Christian doctrine, and to show, on the other, the veritable historical evil it produced in the world.

We have indicated several causes of degeneracy in the Christian **ethics:** the abolition of the **Law, the** fiction of the death and resurrection of the faithful with Jesus, the state of innocence to which **we** are restored by the virtue of Jesus, the theory of the Law begetting sin, and the externality of the redemption and atonement. We are about to see these causes successively beget some one of those monstrous doctrines that stain the history of Christianity, and have no possible parallel in the history of the Synagogue, just because they were unknown in Judaism. And the very language of the sects themselves will show unequivocally the logical connection of effect with cause, which we have assigned.

No more precipitate blossoming can be imagined. As early as the Apostolic times even, the seeds sown in Christian soil puts forth its foul, dark-hued buds. Though it produced at that time excessive vices, crimes and disorders, this, still, would not be so bad, nor prove, withal, the truth of our deductions, if those vices and excesses were not, thenceforth systematized and did not get a scientific precision, a theory, a justification, I was about to say, a formal *consecration*. What constitutes their importance and what unfortunately makes us right on all points is, that those vices did not hide themselves, were not ashamed, that they boldly established themselves in the Church, that they shamelessly displayed their deformity in open day, and that they deemed themselves justified by Christian dogma and ethics. This is what cannot be disputed and what constitutes for us the vital point of the question. We are hardly surprised, much less scandalized, to hear from the mouth of the Apostle that there were in the Church *fornicators, idolaters, adulteresses, effeminate persons, sinners against nature, thieves, covetous people, drunkards, extortioners;** that there were among the Christians impurities unknown to the Gentiles; that a Christian cohabited with his father's wife : all this, unhappily, is in so much accord with human nature that Christianity cannot, without flagrant injustice, be held responsible. But the motive, pretext and occasion of this revolting picture are exclusively its own. Is it not manifest from the words of the Apostle that Christian liberty created those libertines and criminals? Did they not entrench themselves behind the *abolition of the Law?* Did they not avail themselves of Paul's allowing every enjoyment forbidden by Judaism ? And see the Apostle surprised, disconcerted, fighting painfully in this unexpected embarrassment created by himself ! He defends and protects himself as well as he can ; he tries to deaden the blow about to be given him with his own weapons : "*All things,*" says he, "*are lawful for me,*"—here, then, are the words with which this rabble wallowed in the mire of every sin —*but all things* ARE NOT EXPEDIENT : all things are lawful for me—repeating this infelicitous and immoral phrase to abate its force—"*but I will not be brought under the power of any. Meats for the belly and the belly for meats, but God shall destroy both it and them. Now the body is not for fornication, but for the Lord, and the Lord for the body.*" † Vain efforts! Impotent dialectics ! Miserable subterfuges, too late opposed to the cry of *liberty* raised against the Law — the law that sanctioned and protected its ceremonials, no less than its ethics ! Useless pro-

---

* Cor. v. 10, 11, and vi. 10. † Cor. vi. 12, 13.

testation against the vices **and** passions that, chained up before by the Law in the depths of the human heart, rise in their turn, break their fetters-and **shout** liberty ! A glance suffices to detect all that **is false,** embarrassing and illogical in this desperate defence **of Paul's.** He dares not retract the false words, *"All things* **are** *lawful for me."* He has repeated them too often, and they **are too** deeply sunk in the hearts of the faithful for any **human** power to uproot : so he does not attempt it even ; he **can** apply only palliatives. And what palliatives ! *" All things* **are** *lawful for me,* but all things are not *expedient.* What an avowal ! what a degradation ! what a fall ! He dares not speak of virtue, duty, morality in the abstract, to these deluded, brutalized multitudes, he speaks to them of *expediency;* he does not dispute that all is lawful, he denies only that all is *convenient,* and that man, henceforth master of his actions, should make full use of a boundless liberty.

If this expediency were, at least, dictated by reasonable motives ! Paul tries to assign them. He imagines a plausible distinction between the dietary laws and the moral. *Meats are for the stomach, and the stomach for meats, but God shall destroy both. But the body is not for fornication, but for the Lord.* Not one, I dare say, of those great sinners who could not demolish, with **one** stroke, Paul's reasoning, by telling him that if meats are made for the stomach, pleasures are likewise for the body ; that if God must destroy stomach and meats, so must He the hand extended for theft, the arm for homicide, the senses clogged from gluttony, drunkeness, and licentiousness ; that if the body is made for the Lord, it is worth something probably—the care of God for instance ;—that He is not indifferent to its concerns, and that it is not true that whatever goes into the mouth does not defile it, as do theft and adultery. Is it desirable to look further still into the meaning of this *expediency,* that is, henceforth, to constitute Paul's sole safety-plank from the general wreck ? Or to see if we have calumniated the Apostle ? Speaking of meats sacrificed to idols and eaten by many of the faithful,—from which Paul exhorts abstinence in order to avoid scandal,—he uses again his grand phrase, " All is lawful for me, but all is not expedient ; all things are allowed me, but all things do not edify " (1 Cor. x., 23). This additional light upon the value of the term, *expediency,* shows how exactly correct is our explanation. It is not as yet a heresy that has a name, a standard, a history, though it is truly the germ of a heresy. The first historical one that truly bears this name, the oldest example of human reason left to itself in the heart-centre of Christianity, is a grand outburst against morality. No older sect is known than the Nicolaites of whom the Apocalypse speaks (ii., 15) as a heresy whose doctrines were already notorious and wide spread. No obscure person was this Nicolas, the founder of a sect, one of the seven deacons of the Church. A spectacle not a little instructive is that of the Nicolaites, who, at the cradle almost of Christianity, made every sort of licentiousness and immorality their rule of life ; who, the better to escape the slavery of the senses, and not waste the freedom of the soul in constant tiresome struggles, desired to exhaust the flesh by complying with all its desires. Is not this Paul's principle, pushed to the furthest limits? Is not this the natural fruit of a contempt and degradation of the flesh ?

Without leaving the evangelical era and sphere, we meet, furthermore, prophetesses who rivaled in immorality the deacon Nicolas. That old Jew, that noble and pure spirit John, the well-beloved disciple of Jesus, is stirred with a holy zeal against the town that welcomed him and against the bishop who allowed the predictions of the prophetess : *"Angel of the Church at Thyatira,* writes he, ... *I have something against thee ; it is that thou sufferest that Jezabel, who calls herself a prophetess, to teach and seduce my servants to commit fornication and to eat things sacrificed to idols."* Here appears the same licentiousness against which Paul contended.

Do we need to review here the long list of Gnostic sects? The oldest is that of the Simonians, the direct brood of Simon, called the magician, a contemporary of the Apostles, who did not affirm that good works were needless for salvation. After him came a crowd of imitators. Without mentioning the Nicolaites to whom we have alluded, there were the Valentinians who denied the necessity of good works, and deemed their salvation sure by being only *spiritual* or pneumatic. There were the Basilideans, the Cainites, and the Carpocratians who pushed their spirituality still further, by making the most flagrant violation of all morality and incumbent duty : the Actians or Eunomians, who likewise denied the necessity of good works. In the fourth century came the Messalians, who gave the faithful a dispensation from every virtue, provided they prayed incessantly, and who, having become as they thought incapable of sin, abandoned themselves without scruple to all kinds of licentiousness. Prior to these, in the second century, were the Adamites, who pretended that they had been restored by Jesus to the original innocence of Adam, and who consequently went naked, rejected marriage, and deemed the community of women a privilege of this return to primitive innocence. Then in the middle ages was a swarm of monstrous sects. The one last mentioned begot in the twelfth century the sect of Teudemus, who declared fornication and adultery holy and meritorious ; in the fourteenth, the Turlupins who maintained that when man had arrived at a certain point of perfection, he was freed from all law, and that the liberty of the sage consisted, not in ruling his passions, but on the contrary, in shaking off the yoke of the divine laws. We need not relate what abominable practices followed such theories. Finally, at the commencement of the fifteenth century the Picards or Begghaws renewed all the errors of the old Adamites. The middle ages produced also the Brothers of the Free Soul, who maintained the unimportance of external works.

We cannot leave the middle ages without making two remarks which the intelligent reader will appreciate. One has particular reference to the Gnostics. We see in their systemized depravity, a confirmation, from point to point, of our assertion—that this sort of error and licentiousness originates in the contempt of the body preached by Christianity. We said before that this could be exhibited in two ways ; either by mortifying one's body by subjecting it to the most severe privations, or in refusing it everything, *even rule itself*. We have also said that this fiction, the dream of the new-birth era, of a perfection unexampled in this life, was calculated to craze people on the subject of morals, and to authorize acts, criminal, doubtless, under existing physical and moral conditions, but not so under the imaginary ones of that unreal kingdom to which they believed themselves admitted.

Is it not this that we see among the Gnostics ? Are not these the exact causes we see in play ? Was it not this contempt of the body that produced among them the two at once opposite effects in the one case, a rule of life excessively rigid, unheard of mortifications; in the other, a boundless disorder and unparalleled enormities ?

The other remark is no less important, and we have had elsewhere occasion to make a similar one, respecting the protestations renewed from age to age in Christendom, against the distinction of *persons* in the Deity.

We should say then: Since Monotheism,—in spite of the double influence of ancient Paganism (eminently polytheistic), in spite of the influence of authorative Christianity, in spite of the tendency and general character of the age,—yet penetrated through all obstacles, its germ must indeed have originally lain in Christianity, though stifled afterwards by those parasitical Gnostics that usurped its place and hindered its expansion. We make the same assertion of the present time, and doubtless with more reason still. If, in spite of the moral instincts of all rational creatures, and of their innate notions of right and wrong; in spite of Pagan morals which, though corrupt indeed as well, yet never dared raise that corruption to the dignity of a principle, or systematize and consecrate immorality; if in spite of the example, the authority, and the condemnations of official Christianity these errors made way; if there is no period in the history of the Church when the eye is not saddened by some revolting spectacle, by some monstrous theory; if these sects, in the fifteenth century even, made full display of their hideous nudity ; and lastly, if Judaism, in the numerous phases of its history immovably secular, never astonished the world by similar spectacles,—we must indeed say that Christianity contained some latent force, some powerful germ, that strove irresistibly to grow, to expand, and to bear plenteous fruit. And what is this germ, if not the very causes we have named?

We have just said that Judaism is free from such stains. We hasten to add that there is a single exception, which also goes to prove, not only the nature of the errors that produced such effects, but even the Cabalistic origin of Christianity,—an origin that through the corruption of doctrine, contributed powerfully to the birth and growth of this abominable morality. This exception is another *pretended Messiah*, another Cabalist. His name was Schabbatai Zevi. Instructive sight! With him the same sequence, the same connection of doctrines ends in the same abominations. He, too, is the *incarnate righteousness* of God; he, too, is the God-Messiah, the introducer of a new era, who opens, in his own person, the Messianic age, the world to come. He, too, distinguishes the Spiritual from the Psychics and the Hylics, because the Zohar seemed to authorize it; only he does not interpret this spirituality according to the Zohar, but truly after Paul's fashion ; he, too, lives in this world of spirituality and perfect liberty which is the *Bina*, the superior mother, the world to come, where evil is not perceptible even, where no distinction separates the pure from the impure, good from evil, because there all is good, pure and beautiful ; he, too, living in this fantastic world, thinks all is lawful for him, and Messiah, Saint, God though he styles himself, he astonishes the world by his unspeakable impurities, his open licentiousness, shameless, I was about to say religious, since it was in the name of religion, duty and virtue that he transgressed. Is it not, as we have elsewhere said, a history in miniature (better known as it is nearer us) of the birth and vicissitudes of Christianity?

Another consideration already touched on, throws still more light on the importance of these examples. It is that whenever Christianity **thought found** itself uncontrolled, whenever this great tree, **instead of** vegetating in official enclosures, under the artificial **heat** its guardians meted out to it, could freely expand **to the free** air and sunlight, it failed not to produce, close to its **finest** shoots, most agreeable fruits, and healthiest shades, a **branch**, a fruit, a shade of death, as say the Scriptures : as witness **two** great epochs of Christian history. The first, its virgin liberty, unbroken as yet to ecclesiastical authority, namely *Gnosticism*, of which we have spoken; the other, its reconquered liberty, the yoke of the exterior Church for the first time shaken off, namely Protestantism, about which we shall say a few words. Will Protestantism confirm our predictions ? What will this reassertion of the right of free inquiry, this return to strict reason, this appeal to good sense, logic, and the free interpretation of Scripture produce ? **Beyond** doubt, if the same phenomenon show itself, if **the same** immorality come to crown efforts so **great,** aspirations so noble, and independence so proud ; if this is **the final** result of all free investigation, we must say that the germs and causes I have pointed out, lie absolutely at the root of Christianity. And remember that Protestantism, sounding **the** reveille for our paralyzed or dormant faculties, naturally allies itself with all the noble and generous instincts of the heart; **it makes** its appearance in history at a time comparatively **advanced,** when morals began to throw off that gross mould, acquired during the middle ages, and when classic studies aided the parallel development of our better faculties. What better omens could be desired of the advent of a pure and high morality? And yet, what a harrowing picture does the religion of a free enquiry present ! Far from reproaching Protestantism, we say that it has completely fulfilled its mission, that it has unhesitatingly and courageously laid bare the defects in Christian ethics and the evil it may produce when the sacerdotal eye no longer **keeps** watch over the threatening hydra. But, however, our assertions are only better proved, and the history of Protestant doctrine is our strongest support.

Facts speak for themselves. We shall but mention John Huss, who obeying his personal inspiration alone, teaches the same doctrine. But Luther comes ; he frees himself from the ruling church, and does not recoil from the most audacious revolt. What will he decide as to ethics. What will be his judgment on good works ? One, I dare say, that will cause a shudder. He pronounces them *mortal sins*. Reason, the heart, good morals, oppose this doctrine through Melancthon. Vain resistance! In 1567 the Diet of Worms condemns him and approves of Luther's ethics. Can we expect anything better of Calvin? He has, nevertheless, no connexion with any one, neither with Luther, nor the church. What will he teach regarding Christian ethics? "*We believe*," say the Calvanists in chorus, "*that by faith alone we share the righteousness of Jesus Christ;* GOD HAS NO REGARD FOR GOOD WORKS. Protestantism passes from hand to hand, changes its schools, its masters, its country, its church—its morality is always the same. The Anglicans, who are the most moderate, announce in 1562: *That good works, the products of faith even, cannot expiate our sins and satisfy the strict justice of God. . . . . As to those done without the grace of Jesus, they are but mortal sins.*"

Years glide away, and we pass to another form of Protestantism, to another country: and the ethics? *Moral works*, says the Calvanistic synod of 1618, *do not count for our justification*. We are almost on the threshold of modern times, and the Christian ethics, with free speech, free teaching, has not budged a step.

Let us, however, imitate the sick man who shifts his position to ease his pain: let us pass to another church, let us ask from another period information about the Catholic morality. Remarkable fact! While the priesthood, ever on the alert, half religious, half secular, watches over Catholic morality lest it should stray to paths, where society might be lost with it, the breath of liberty, the spirit of philosophy, logic and its claims, penetrate through those gratings, those iron walls that a compact hierarchy oppose to their entrance; and one fine day, in this enclosure so guarded, ruled and watched, a strange exotic plant shoots forth, the germs of which doubtless lay in the lowest strata of the soil, but which a more penetrating sun-ray, a breath of spring quite fresh, has caused to blossom, to the astonishment of the guardians. We need hardly say we allude to *Quietism*. Molinos who has given it for ever his name, bold as he was, is not isolated in the history of Catholicism. He belongs to the school that claims Origen as father, and that survived in Evager, deacon of Constantinople, in the Hesychastes of the 14th century, in the Begghards (who carried doctrinal consequences further), and to a greater or less degree in most of the Mystics, the most celebrated of whom, in this respect, was the archbishop of Cambray. Now the most characteristic doctrine of Quietism, that upon which, far or near, were based all the forementioned schools, and which awoke the alarm of the church was: That, *in the contemplative state, the use of sacraments and the practice of good works, are unimportant* **matters,** *and that the most criminal pictures and impressions that are formed on the sensitive part of the soul* **are not sins.** Fenelon himself, archbishop and moderatist as he **was,** this candid, noble soul and loyal Catholic, did not deem that he was erring from the truth by teaching that the soul may, without guilt, push its disinterestedness to the point that it is no longer solicitous about its salvation or damnation; and the Society of the Holy-Office had need of *thirty-seven* conferences to censure Fenelon.

Thus every blow aimed by Christianity against ancient Jewish orthodoxy recoiled against the most sacred interests of morality and shook its most natural supports.

Christianity, placing its kingdom out of this world, not taking in political society, condemning the secularity of the Mosaic system, was forced from the nature of things, to mount itself the empty throne, to choose servitude or dominion, to put the spiritual in the place of the temporal, and, with the same stroke, to establish religious intolerance. By the abolition of the law, it sapped the foundations of morality; it prepared and authorized, unwittingly no doubt, licentiousness of morals. By its fictions about death and resurrection, forced suppositions for a reality negatived by fact, it sanctioned the huge humbug of *giving to the living the liberty of the dead,* to existing humanity the laws that shall rule it when it leaves the tomb. By the Redemption, it exerted a triple influence upon the fate of morality: by the restoration of man to Adam's primitive state, it consecrated a retrospective fiction, just as by the fiction of the resurrection it forestalled the rights of the most distant future—an illusion as great in the one case as in the other! By its very idea of sin, it overturned the most natural notions of right and wrong, teaching that it is through the Law alone we are made acquainted with *sin.* By the very act of redemption it detached man from the work of salvation, by throwing upon the God-Messiah all the weight of expiation, and transferring the sphere of his regeneration from within to without. In a word, the pernicious fruits of these speculative errors were not slow to appear—what do I say— did not cease to manifest themselves from age to age in numberless and learned heresies, strange apparitions doubtless, often frightful and detestable, but which the logical sequence of ideas brought from time to time upon the stage of history, the subjects at once of terror, indignation and mournful thought, for generations to come.

CHAPTER IV.

CHRISTIAN ETHICS.

Its Titles and its Pretentions.—Why Hebrew Ethics has not been duly Appreciated.—Division of Ethics.—Dignity of Man, his Fall, his Regeneration.—Free Judgment and Grace.—Life.—General Maxims.—Pharisaical plan.—Examples.—Testimony of the Gospels.

We judged that we could not proceed in our essay on Christian ethics better than by commencing with an examination of the theoretic foundations upon which this rests. Have we erred in our choice of method? Or have we, by chance, gone astray in our estimations? The reader must say.

However that be, another work, a new task awaits us. Whatever be the foundation of Christian ethics, whatever may be decided against their solidity, still a grand and imposing structure has been raised upon them. A thousand generations have been sheltered beneath its hospitable roof; a thousand sufferings and griefs have found there an almost divine alleviation; a thousand virtues have spread from it through the world, everywhere inspiring courage for the good, fear for the evil; a thousand intellects have bent in reverence before it; let us too bend before this masterpiece of half a dozen Jews, before this branch of the great Hebrew tree, grafted on the trunk of the Gentiles. We recognize there the footprints of Judaism, the spirit of the patriarchs, prophets and doctors; and are tempted to say with old Isaac: "Truly the hands are Esau's, but the voice is indeed Jacobs'."

Deplorable effect of an ever widening breach! It happened, however that, after many ages, Christianity and Judaism tired, the one of smiting, the other of suffering, met one day, and recognized each other, saluting with the address of father and son. But, O shame! the son did not bow before the white hair of his father, the father neither embraced nor blessed his son, the Joseph, whom, torn so young from the paternal hearth, he found in Egypt, great, rich, proud of his power. Whose the fault? History will say, when the father and son, reconciled, shall embrace.

Meantime, if there be anything which retards the advent of that great day, it is the superiority the son arrogates over his old father,—Christianity over the religion of Israel—as regarding morality. If there be any outrage which a father cannot endure without degradation, it is assuredly this. To truth, criticism and opinion, we leave the task of examining this pretension, and of terminating a demeanor that has prevailed for ages. Many a time, alas! Judaism **has had to bear** the stigma of this insult, and many a time **has it** realized the terrible prediction of Isaiah, that persecution **would add** slander **to a** secular martyrdom. Shall **a day of justice,** of impartiality, of right criticism ever come? **Let us** hope so. Already learned pens have wrought at the **great** work; already is opinion moved, shaken, and open **criticism** speaks of certain Jewish maxims (as the well **known reply of** Hillel to the proselyte) that preceded and inspired the founder of Christianity. Why it has not yet won a just **and lawful** victory, and why a full success has not crowned such efforts, **we** shall frankly tell. It is from two causes equally deplorable. The one, that a sufficient line of demarcation has not been drawn between Jewish civil polity and its ethics proper, an indispensable distinction, absolutely required, from the two fold nature of Judaism, as we have shown. **The** other, that too little **importance** has been **attached to** tradition, though I grant that the harangues of a hostile camp, **or an** affectation of Jewish Puritanism, not at all in **accord** with the traditional, rabbinical Judaism we profess, has given it sufficient. We shall do our best to avoid **these two rocks;** happy if we advance even one step this religious question, which, though not debated in the civil courts or journals, beats deeply, nevertheless, in the heart and brain of man.

We shall divide our work into several parts. Our starting point shall be *man*, the ideas that each side entertains respecting **him, its** ideas, also, of the world and life, and the general maxims that both have laid down, respecting morals. The **duties that** regard ourselves, humility, innocence, truth, self-denial, **voluntary** poverty; the duties that we owe **to** others, and above all, *charity*, that great word, which Christianity pronounced for the first time to an ignorant world; the forgiveness of injuries; love towards one's enemies; our ideas about sinners, the anxiety they cause; forbearance;—the duties, in fine, that connect us with God: the aim of our actions, the glory of God, **faith,** trust in God, love of God and perseverance,—such are the grand subjects that shall occupy us a little while, too sure that we cannot exhaust the least of them. But it will suffice, **if we** throw on each such light as may guide some one of greater power and inspiration to a complete performance.

In speaking of man, we shall here take occasion to state once more that to Judaism, unquestionably, belongs the glory of having first announced to men that they are children of the same father; of having, in a word, proclaimed a UNIVERSAL BROTHERHOOD. We believe that this glory will not be dimmed, if it **takes precedence of** that charity, whose brightest jewel and firmest stay it is. Nor shall we speak of the soul and its powers, and scarcely shall we touch, in passing, on free judgment and original sin. We do not discourse on the whole nature of man, but only on what has direct reference to practical morality.

Now, man's dignity possesses for man a most powerful attraction. Doubtless the Gospels have some traits that exalt to his view human nature, although other views and particularly ulterior theological speculations have placed him far beneath those calm hights to which Judaism had raised him. If we read in Luke that the kingdom of God is within us, if there is nothing more frequent than to hear the faithful called "members of Christ," if they will have it that "Christ dwells in us," if the believer ranks with the angels and even above them,—this, when well understood, is only the lost echo of ancient Jewish doctrines, that were yet alive in the days of Jesus. Judaism, as we know, declares man made after the image of God; he is the king and master of creation, he is the vicar and providence of God upon earth—I had almost said he was its God, as, according to the Rabbis, God said to Jacob, "I am God above, thou art god below." He is, according to the Midrasch, the love-knot uniting heaven and earth, for he has the spiritual nature of the one, and the corporeal nature of the other; by this precious combination he makes peace between the spirit and the body, between heaven and earth—ever at variance. And if we question the Cabalists about this, they tell us that man's influence, his thoughts, sentiments and actions have an echo and vibrate sensitively, like the rings of some subtle, delicate chain, in the farthest spheres of the universe. But what is this in-dwelling *Kingdom of God* if not the present Pharisaism? Moses said: "Build me a tabernacle that I may dwell in the midst of them." The Rabbis go much farther: by a slight and felicitous modification, of which the Mosaic words are quite susceptible, they change this wooden tabernacle, where God is about to dwell, to the soul, heart, and spirit of man,—a house a thousand times more worthy of Deity—and they make this great assertion, that *God dwells in Israel, within him.* This, however, is only the simple germ which we must see in its rich and powerful bloom from the hands of the Cabalists. This miserable body of man is nothing less than an august temple, whose parts are his members; and taking with one hand the plan of the Temple of Jerusalem, with the other, the *descriptive anatomy* of the human body, they trace, step by step, the parallel development of each, assigning to each member a function corresponding to some part of the Temple, and they end at last with this sublime statement, that *the heart is* **the Holy of** *Holies*, or the special and usual seat of the Glory (SCHECHINA), **which** is nothing else than the kingdom of God, **as we have** frequently affirmed, and as the passage from Luke **plainly shows.** Much more; the just man is the *car* the **true car,** that **God** guides, and the soul of the just **is** at once the **car and** the throne of his holiness.

We are—all of us—members of the Schechina, of **the** **Kingdom (as** the faithful are members of Jesus, the incarnate Word); **and** this is why all suffering and pain react on the heart of this tender mother, who fails not to moan at each blood drop or tear **of** even the impious, and to show herself wounded by the same stroke that has smitten **a** member-child.* After this shall we be surprised to hear **the** doctors **and** cabalists **say** that human souls are superior to angels, **as the** protected is superior to the protector; that they **were** the counselors **of God at the time of** the creation; that the **just are God's** coadjutants in forming the heavens and the earth; **that they too have** the title creators; that they are the support **and foundation of the** universe; **that** the angels will one day **ask the just to** disclose the mysteries **of** the eternal—which **Paul expresses in** his fashion by saying: "Know ye not, that we **shall judge** the angels;" † and which Peter also teaches, saying **that the** angels desire **to** look into the Gospel prediction (1 Gen. **Ep. i.** 12)—that they rise to such a degree of holiness that the **angels shall** proclaim them thrice holy, as they do the Creator; **and that, at** last, God will deign to allow them His incom**municable name.** Here, indeed, is an ideal, beyond imagination noble, attractive and sublime. Add, that all can attain this end; that each one may aspire to equal Moses or Aaron, AND THAT HE OUGHT—and we can see what grand perspectives Judaism opens for the observant believer, and what superior ardor must animate the most apathetic soul, in the presence of a future so glorious, of possibilities so strange.

Nevertheless, man' is **fallen; this** Judaism as well as **Chris**tianity teaches, with **this** difference always, that, in **the** Genesaic history of the Fall, the former gives us glimpses **of** a philosophy, far different **in** sense from the childish story **of** the apple **and** the serpent, while Christianity, on the contrary, ever regards **sin,** true sin, **as** the result of **the** unlucky fruit presented to Adam, and the Church shut the mouth of Origen, who tried to **lift** himself a little beyond the literal sense. In Judaism, every school of any importance, from the Cabalists downward, sees **in** the narrative of Genesis something above and beyond the drama **of** Paradise. Still, with all man is fallen; and

* Sanhederin, 46.   † 1 Cor. vi. 3.

how shall he rise? By the incarnate word, replies Christianity; by the incarnate Word, likewise replies Judaism and especially Cabalistic Judaism. But what is this *incarnate Word?* Here it is, that the diverse genius of each religion shows itself to every eye.

The Word, says Christianity, the eternal Logos, becomes flesh; is born, lives, speaks, teaches, sacrifices himself as a sin-expiation; and all mankind suffer, die, rise with him, and through him recover their primitive purity. *Incarnation, sacrifice, virtue, merit, atonement,* all quite exterior things, are applied to mankind by a single word, and that is IMPUTATION. Is it the same in Cabalistic Judaism? There, the Word, Logos, Tipheret, besides its eternal incarnation as *substance* in nature, incarnates itself also as *thought* in the Law; law, which under a thousand phases and a thousand applications, governs the universe, from the angel before God or the star that rolls in infinite space, to the worm that creeps on the earth, to man who is included also in the universal harmony, and for whom this thousand-faced, thousand-sided law circumscribes itself, adapts itself to the plan he occupies in creation, and becomes the *law of Moses*. This is the Word, the incarnate Law—this is the perpetual Eucharist upon which the holy feed, and this the redemption that has for its sphere the heart and mind of man—the Law, the Sinai, at the foot of which the Israelites were cleansed from the old stain of our first parents. We need not dwell upon the pernicious effects of a redemption quite external, offered us by Christianity; we have seen them but too well in all those fore-mentioned schools or heresies, that justified their apathy or licentiousness by the stupefaction of the moral faculties inevitably produced by the Christian theory of redemption. How, if we enter for a moment the sanctuary of conscience, and ask Christianity what use it has made of free judgment, the most precious, unquestionably, of God's gifts? Far are we from wishing to involve ourselves in that dark labyrinth where *graces* of every sort are so lavished, that human liberty is at last stifled beneath the weight of so many benefits. If any fact come clearly forth from that grand discussion, dating from the birth of Christianity and continued almost to our day, it is, that with the Catholics (who, after all, grant the largest field to human liberty), man is led to good, to virtue, only through an inciting influence from on high. This is the decision of the Council of Orange in 529, against the semi-Pelagiens. What does Judaism teach about grace, and free Judgment? Doubtless it, too, recognizes the action of God upon man's liberty, it believes in a co-operation through which we are aided to rise towards Him. Doubtless it, too, offers a continual prayer for this grace, **this invaluable** help. But, let us haste to add, that the only **doctrine at the** roots of Christianity that is a true reflection of **old Jewish** orthodoxy is that one qualified by semi-Pelagianism. If nothing perfect can be accomplished by man without **the** aid of the Eternal; if He alone imparts courage, light, **and** perseverance to man's heart,—the first step withal, the **initiative** of every good work, the first aspiration towards good**ness**, truth and ineffable beauty must spring from the heart itself **of** man. He, himself, as say the doctors, must open to them the door,—were this but as small as a needle's point,—in order that God may throw open for him another as wide as the Temple's; * and to sum all with a Cabalistic saying: "*The arousal is, first, from below, then from above.*"

Is not this to augment at once the responsibility and the grandeur of man?—to make him, instead of a passive instrument in God's hands, a force to which He has assigned its own sphere of action?—to condemn, in the same sentence, idleness, dissipation and neglect of duty?—and to give an increased impulse to man, who needs **but** a simple noble beginning to see himself instantly penetrated with light, courage and invincible strength—priceless gifts from **on** high. Man, about whom are such conflicting ideas, is cast on this earth, the theatre of his acts, under the mysterious conditions we call *life*. What idea does Christianity give us of life? **It** would be easy to appeal here to those great geniuses, ancient and modern, who have seen in Christianity, hate of the world, condemnation of life, contempt of all its charms and most precious gifts. **Our** task would be too easy, and we might seem to take refuge under imposing names. Doubtless a testimony almost unanimous would be no small presumption in favor of what we have said, and are about to say; but it is from the Gospels that we wish to ask the theory of life, the ideas we ought to entertain of the world, of its values, its conditions and its relations to life eternal. Now, if there be anything proveable in the Gospels it is that the term *world*, invariably figures there as the synonym of vice, evil and sin. Could it be otherwise with a religion that terms itself exiled here below, and that cries: My kingdom is not of this world!

Indeed, it would be an endless task to examine and cite all the passages where the *world* is made the antithesis of virtue; and the transformation this word has undergone—to stand as the symbol of evil, instead of the Hebrew synonym of eternity (olam)—is not the least injury Jewish thought has

* Midrasch Shirhashirim.

suffered at the hand of Christianity. We shall say only that what happened to the *Law*, has happened to the *world*. We have seen that the Law was identified with sin, and the world also is to be identified with it, with evil. Some decisive quotations will suffice to confirm the assertions of the most impartial criticisms. Jesus told his disciples that *they were not of the world*, even as he was not of the world;* and what proves that no interpretation but the most absolute and literal is admissible, is that the PRINCE OF THIS WORLD is always represented as the adversary of Jesus and his Church. And truly, it is impossible to say that the word *world* refers merely to the generation of that time, or yet again to what is evil and vicious here below. For the genius of evil would never have been personified by "the Prince of this world," if the world itself had not appeared to Jesus and his followers worthy only of the rule of a demon. See John xii. 31,— where *the Prince of this world* is about to be "cast out,"—and chapter xiv. 30,—where the Prince of this world advances against Jesus to destroy him—and the justness of our assertion, and of the opinion of Marcion (heretic though he was), will be seen, namely, that the God of the ancient law, though truly the God of Nature as well, is yet very different from the Deity of the Gospels.

With Judaism it is altogether different. We do not say the Judaism of the Bible; for, so far from falling into the extravagance of the Gospels, it seems to lean rather to the other side, in so favorable a light are presented the actual world, life, its worth, and conditions; and the inferential denial that it has any spirituality, any regard for another life, is the proof of this. So we shall imitate Mr. Salvador, who, following the Bible only, sees in Judaism nothing but *matter* and material advantages, in other words, a complete antithesis to the Christian conception. No! true Judaism lies not here, but in *tradition* and its instruments, that, while accepting the heritage of the Bible, dominate it, from the full hight and superiority of eternal life, upon this ephemeral orb. Now, how speaks tradition regarding *the world?* It is not a prison, a hell, a purgatory, a place of banishment, as the religious or philosophic alternately teach. It is simply a *vestibule*. No longer *the highroad*, but not as yet *the house;* it is a place of initiation, of apprenticeship to a future life, where the guests prepare to enter the *triclinium* or dining-hall palace.†
It is the *to-day*, as eternity is the *to-morrow;* the time for labor, for action, for good works, for worship and piety, as eternity is the time for *retribution;*‡ it is the eve of the Sabbath, on which

---

* John, xvii.   † Aboth, chap. iv.   ‡ Tal., treatise Eroubin, chap. ii.

the repast is prepared **for the Lord's Day**;* it **is** the season of duty and submission, **as the morrow** shall be **that** of freedom from every law.† **Precious time!** "wherein a single hour of virtue **and repentance is** worth more than an entire eternity," for the **latter** gives only in the degree that it receives;‡ and not **without** reason did Solomon pronounce the dead lion less **happy** than the living dog.∥

One fact gives the whole difference between the two **doctrines,** namely, that while the *Prince of this world* is, for Christianity, **the** genius of evil, this title is given by the Cabalists to their kingdom, the *Malchout*, also styled the Prince of this world. A fact doubly significant! for while, on the one hand, it confirms our judgment on the present question, it makes us almost see the moral consequences of that omission in dogma of which we have spoken, I mean the obliteration and absorption of the *Malchout* (the present world), **into** the heart of the Bina (the world to come). In the place so made void, Christianity has enthroned a *demon—the Prince of this world.*

We shall but point out what renders Christianity incapable of governing the present life, condemning, spurning **and** vilifying as it does all its most precious gifts. Life itself **is** an incumbrance, **a** weight, of which **we** should desire to be quickly **rid (Paul); the** flesh, is "a flesh of sin," that can be reinstated only by death and resurrection. Could it find a place for the dearest **and** holiest affections? The rich and riches, the great, and all human grandeur, science, joy, get not a word indicative of the good use to which man may convert them here below. I know well that the Church tries hard to see, in the anathematizing of this use, a condemnation of abuses only. In **vain!** for not only does John exhort **us not to** love the world or the things it contains,§—he who loves it is not loved of God: in the world all is concupiscence of the flesh, **lust** of the eyes and pride of life,—but Jesus himself cries to **us,**¶ "Woe to ye, rich men!" On account of their vices? **No;** *"because ye have already had your consolation."* "Woe to **ye** that are filled!" And why? Because a reverse of fortune awaits them? No; *"because ye shall hunger."* "Woe to ye that laugh now, for ye shall lament and weep." **Could** there be a place for love? Doubtless charity is recommended; but those special and no less sacred ties, that adorn and sanctify life will be lost, I dare say, effaced and dissolved in universal charity, in the Church.

---

* Talmud, Aboda **Zara, chap. i.**
† Talmud, Schbabat, **chap. ii.**
‡ Aboth, *loc. cit.*
∥ Talmud, Schabbat, *l, c.*
§ John, chap. i.
¶ Luc., chap. vi.

And first, could anything good, lawful or sacred exist in this world, this life, this sinful flesh, without being infected by nature and sharing their condemnation?

Could it be the family? But, *he who will not leave father, mother, brothers, sisters, to follow the new doctrine shall not have done his whole duty;* nor can the performance of even the last office for a parent make the disciple of Jesus relent a mite, for it is *the dead who must bury their dead.* Jesus himself, when told that his mother, brothers and sisters were waiting for him at the door: "These," said he, turning to his disciples, "are my mother, brothers and sisters;" and so well did he thenceforth identify himself with the era of the resurrection which, to his view, was also that of the Messiah, that he dares to say to his mother: "*Woman, what have I to do with thee?*" Is this the spectacle that Judaism presents? With it the family is not only the central point from whose expansion must come the state, but the domestic hearth is the first temple, the first altar for worship, and the model it gives us for imitation, is the patriarch surrounded by his family, adoring and sacrificing to the Most High.

Could it be marriage? We shall not repeat the assertion that the Gospel condemns it; but it is indisputable that neither Jesus nor his apostles encourage or bless it, and the most that we can infer from the words of Paul is but the simple toleration of an evil with which he could not wholly do away.

Thus life, health, riches, science, honor, glory, love, family, country, all that make existence great, holy and happy, these reflections of heaven below, the reminiscences of paradise, these foretastes of eternity, all vilified, spurned and sacrificed to that prospective life, to that kingdom *not of this world,*—all swept away by the same torrent that bore off into the region of dogma whatever gave value and position, in the divine economy, to the things of time—the *kingdom,* the *Malchout,* which is of this world indeed, nay—is the world itself (Olam haze) with which Jesus, by an unmistakable allusion, contrasts another *kingdom not of this world.*

Whatever be the value of life, of this world, of the existing society, in them man lives, and consequently should have some rule of conduct with respect to them; this rule is Morality. Let us haste to recognize it. The more Christianity subtracts from the private affections, and the more miserly it is at its roots, so much the richer and more lavish is it towards those general affections which the increase and concentration of the human race call forth, and it gives to the *Church,* to *humanity,* all that it takes from *man, family* and *country*. Must **we** not expect this? Is it not **most natural that** a religion announcing itself a stranger to **this world, should** exert its influence and lavish its benefits upon **the** abstractions and generalities of this very world, upon **those lights that divide** heaven **from** earth? In these regions, however, Christianity has a morality, **a** grand morality. But **is it unknown** or superior to that **of** Judaism? Must the **master, after** having given the pupil all, learn from him the **very** things that constitute his forte and speciality—the world, **life,** and humanity?

We shall soon examine in detail the greatest virtues that **have** illustrated the teachings of Christianity. **For** the present we shall confine ourselves to general rules. Like all religions and philosophies, Christianity has general maxims or principles that seem the special features, the germs, **the** creative elements of its whole moral **code. Judaism,** as we are about see, is rich, very rich in generalizations **of this** kind. Everything, to the passage giving the Christian fundamental **rule, shows** this. On what occasion does **Jesus give** the summary **of the** whole law in *the love of God and man?* When the scribe, **who** had heard him **dispute,** asked **him,** *which is the great commandment in the law?* —a question indicating a habit of generalization on the part of the scribe—then Jesus replied: *Thou shalt love the Lord thy God, &c. . . .* And the second resembles the first: *Love thy neighbor as thyself.** An analogous passage occurs **in** Matthew **vii. 12**: "Whatever ye would **that** men do to **you, do** ye likewise to them, for this is the Law and the **Prophets."** Now is this method unknown to Judaism? Can the Gospel illustrations, **in its echos from the** Bible, compete for beauty, grandeur and holiness, with those given us by traditional Judaism? Have we no maxims, no examples **to** vie with **the** Christian ethics, and which can both **explain the** origin of those very Gospel ideas, and establish with **still** greater certainty **the** superiority **of** Hebrew ethics? **The reader** will answer for himself these **questions.** In the monuments **of** tradition, these recapitulations **of** the **law,** these general maxims comprehending all the parts with **all** their beauties, **frequently** occur. We shall spare the reader **these** precepts thus crowning the **law** as its full and last expression—the Sabbath, for example, the tzitzit, and many others. We shall limit ourselves to those—the most numerous —that are exclusively moral, and that are, according to the doctors, the key-stone of the law; not that they ever intended to subordinate and perhaps sacrifice, after the fashion of Jesus, the

* Mark, xxii., 28-31.

ceremonial law to the purely rational ethics, but because they regarded the latter as the *base*, the indispensable condition of a greater elevation; just as in physics, animal life, instinct, good sense, reason, genius, are the several steps of a ladder that we must use in succession to reach safely a summit. This is exactly the Cabalistic theory taught by R. Isaac Louria's greatest disciple in his *Schaari Kedouscha*, and, several centuries before, under somewhat more philosophic influences, by the author of Cozri. However, this method, these maxims abound with the doctors. And, what is remarkable, they not only make more admirable ones for themselves, but they carry the chain of their tradition, exclusively ethical of this generalizing process, back to the prophets, any one of whom almost, would have compressed the whole series of God's commands into a few striking maxims In this way would David present the whole law in eleven commandments: "Aim at perfection, do justice, speak truth according to your mind, slander not, injure no one, be not ashamed of your relations, be humble, honor those who fear God, swear to your own hurt and keep your oath, take no usury, take no bribe to destroy the innocent." And similarly Isaiah reduced the number to six: " Be just, speak rightly, shun unlawful gains, touch not a bribe, listen not to counsel for blood, look not at vice." And Micah simplifies still further the rules of salvation: "O man, what does God require of thee? To do justice, to love mercy, and to walk humbly with Him." Are we done? Not yet. Amos advanced a step, and summed the whole law *in a single precept*, which indeed has a strong resemblance to Paul's system, but, to our view, simply a literal one; namely FAITH.*
And should the great Moses have been less synthetic than his disciples? "Do you remember" say the Pharisees, "when Moses said to Israel: 'You shall follow your God the Everlasting,' Israel replied: 'Who can walk the paths of the Eternal?' Is it not written, 'The whirlwind and the tempest go before him.'" And Moses replied, "No; I shall show you the ways of the Eternal; all his ways are *charity* and *truth*."† Let us pass to the doctors themselves. Should they be inferior to the prophets, to the examples set before them? *We shall see.* Simeon, the Just, prior by several centuries to the Master of Nazarath, and with whom the Rabbinical era just opens, declared (Torah), *religious science, worship* and *charity*, to be the three pillars that sustain all society.‡ Have we not here the archetypes of the three theological Christian virtues, Faith, Hope, and Charity? I incline to think so. The Hebraic genius ever

* Talmud, Maccot, 23.   † Midrash.   ‡ Abbot, chap. i.

shows itself in **this formula.** Like Christianity, assigning to *charity* the highest **rank, it ever associates this** virtue with science and worship; science **(knowledge** of the Law), which tends directly to action, as Hillel **says :** *The ignorant* (boor) *cannot avoid sin*, and his disciples say, **Great** *truly is science that leads to practice;* science that leaves reason all **its** rights ; science, fruitful, active, luminous, instead of that barren, passive, instinctive, not to say blind, faith that rules in Christianity ;—*worship*, pious deeds, but always deeds instead of *hope*, a virtue purely contemplative and idle. Need we relate Hillel's celebrated answer to the proselyte? Criticism has already seized it **and** all know it. Only let us mark two circumstances that appear from a comparison of Hillel's saying with that of Jesus (Mat. vii. **12.**) The thought, as we know, is in both cases the same ; but the form is so too, and especially the closing epiphonemas are very similar. After Hillel said: *What thou dislikest do not to thy neighbor*, he added: *In this is the whole* **Law—Jesus :** *It is the Law and the Prophets.* But while **Jesus (or** perhaps Matthew, on account of the Gentiles, to whom Judaism **was not** to be preached) stops here, Hillel takes care **to add :** *The rest is but the commentary, go and learn it.* This is not all. Christianity, that took this saying from Jewish tradition, imitates the Pharisee Hillel not only in the sense of the doctrine, but also in its application, namely, to evangelize the Gentiles ; for it was to a Gentile, desirous of becoming acquainted with Judaism, that Hillel summed it up in the precept, Love thy neighbor.

But years pass, every thing changes, dies ; country, independence, peace, happiness, liberty—Jewish ethics alone survives unchanged. About two centuries after Hillel we get it once more from the lips of the most distinguished doctors. But what gives special value to the maxims we are about to read, is that their authors were two of the four celebrated doctors who entered Pardis, namely, two masters venerable in cabalistic science, whence Christianity has derived its dogmas and very probably its ethics also—Essenico-Cabalistic ethics. Those doctors are, first, the great Talmudist and **martyr** Akiba, who teaches : *Love thy neighbor as thyself,* **this is the** *great principle of the Law;* and then his colleague, Ben-Azaï, **who** said : **MAN** WAS MADE IN THE IMAGE OF GOD, *this is the great principle of* **the** *Law ; Take care then not to say : As I am made nought of, be my brother also esteemed nought;* **as** *I am cursed, be my brother also cursed;—for if thou doest* **so,** *know that he whom thou despises and curses is the image of God himself.*[*]

We have **seen** from the Gospel itself **(Mark xii.** 28) how the **Pharisees** could **sum** the whole Law **in** general maxims, and we

---

[*] Bereschit Rabba, sect. 24.

shall now see, from the Gospels likewise, the same views exactly respecting those virtues by which the Law was so summed. In Mark as well as in Luke is this clearly shown. In the first, the scribe who comes to question Jesus,—probably to test his doctrine, as many other passages lead us to suppose—after listening to him to the end says (xii. 32, 33): "*Master, thou hast said the truth, that there is but one only God . . . and that to love God with all the soul . . . . and one's neighbor as one's self, is more than all the whole burnt offerings and sacrifices.*" This, surely, is not the language of a man who questioned for instruction, but truly of one who wished to sound the doctrine of another, and who, finding it in accordance with his own ideas, repeats it under the form we have seen. And as far as this *preeminence over holocausts and sacrifices*, there is nothing that does not attest the originality of the Pharisaical maxim, for these are the very terms we find in the Talmud, as we are about to see when speaking of Charity.* The same conclusion, clearer still if possible, comes from Luke,† where the doctor of the Law, instead of questioning Jesus, is questioned himself. It is true that we read (x. 25): "Master, what should I do," &c., TO TEST JESUS, as we are told; which indicates the scribe's object in Mark. But as to the maxim itself, the doctor of the Law in Luke takes it from himself, instead of confining himself to an approval, as in Mark; for when Jesus asks (verse 26): "What is written in the Law?" he answers, "Thou shalt love the Lord thy God, &c., and thy neighbor as thyself;" that is to say, two precepts which, considering the great distance that separates them in the Law (one in Leviticus, the other in Deuteronomy), could not have been brought into contiguity by the doctor if tradition had not anteriorly made them the two inseparable parts of one formula, which the doctor then only repeated for Jesus. Thus the Gospels themselves show the anteriority of generalization and of maxims in the Pharisaical school.

* Charity is greater than all the sacrifices.   † Luke x. 26.

CHAPTER V.

HUMILITY.

ABRAHAM AND MOSES.—THE BIBLE.—THE "POOR IN SPIRIT."—THE KINGDOM AND THE EARTH THAT ARE TO BE THEIR HERITAGE.—CABALISTIC SENSE NECESSARY FOR THE COMPREHENSION OF THE LAW.—GREATNESS OF THE HUMBLE.—AUTHORITY.—EXAMPLE OF JESUS.—SUBMISSION TO INJURY.—OTHER BEATITUDES.—THE PERSECUTED.—PRIDE.—ANGER.—SERPENT AND DOVE.—THE CHILD.—SELF-DENIAL.—VOLUNTARY POVERTY.

If Christian ethics boasts that it taught men charity, it arrogates no less the honor of having taught them humility. It should, however, remember **that the two greatest** Hebrews,—one the spiritual father, the **other** the political **father of** ancient Israel,—are eminently and proverbially **distinguished** for their humility. Abraham esteemed himself but **dust** and **ashes** (Gen. xviii. 27); Moses, as the Scripture states with singular precision, *was the humblest of all men upon the earth:* a phrase well emphasized, and showing the man of God in a light not hitherto sufficiently appreciated, and that invests **him, the first,** with that aureole of goodness and mildness usually ascribed only to the son of Mary. But far from **that,** the latter **is rather a** fiery spirit in an iron mould; he preeminently **possesses** the will, force, and energy that are but apportioned in **the** Hebrew law-giver. We should gain too easy a victory by contrasting **J**udaism with Christianity on the score of humanity. We might turn to the Bible, that abounds in passages where the humble, the meek, the poor in spirit are put at an elevation unknown to the Gospels. But since, as we have said, learned Hebrew writers have fully criticized the Bible, and since Christianity, if not absolutely playing the part of innovator, has so loudly proclaimed its mission as reformer, as restorer of Biblical ethics disfigured by the Pharisees, it is time to sift its claims once for all before another tribunal besides the Church, to wit, that of free Criticism.

When Jesus uttered on the mountain-top these celebrated words: *Happy* **are** *the poor in spirit, for theirs is the kingdom of heaven; Happy* **are** *the meek, for they shall inherit the earth;* and elsewhere: *Learn of me, for I am meek and lowly of heart,* &c., was this anything new for Palestine, anything that was not reechoed each day in its temples, schools, and assemblies? A word first upon the true exposition of the preceding fragments. No doubt but that by "*poor in spirit*" is meant *the humble,* for quite similarly do the Rabbis designate them, *nemoke rouah* (humble in spirit),—from the literal translation of which comes the English phrase—one of the thousand traces of the Rabbinico-Aramean origin of the Gospels. But it is to the promise that ends the verses we would call attention.

In the first, theirs is the *kingdom of heaven;* in the second, *they shall inherit the earth.* The latter, we remark, is but a verse taken from the Psalms (Psl. xxxvii. 11) But is there a real synonym in these expressions? It is very probable that there is, above all if we bear in mind the sense we have given to the Gospel "kingdom of heaven," viz.: that of *Malchout*, the last emanation of the Cabalists, their *kingdom of heaven*. Now, this kingdom seems to be doubly identified with the object of Jesus' promise; first because it takes, in preference to all others, the name *earth*, synonymous with *kingdom*, as Jesus uses it; and again, because this earth, precisely as in the Gospels, is promised by the Cabalists to the meek and humble. And we have but to glance at the Zohar—where a verse almost identical with that of the Psalm, *Tzadikim yireschou aretz*, is interpreted in the same manner, and *aretz*, earth, is said expressly to be the synonym of kingdom—to be assured both as to the sense we here give the Gospel *kingdom*, and as to the synonyms of the Kingdom of verse 3, and the Earth of verse 5. Besides, is it not the most common and well-known doctrine among the Cabalists? Is it not the *Schechina* that is called *anava* (humility),* and which explains Jesus' characteristic *humility*, that other *incarnation*, that other Malchout? Is it not from this that comes inspiration?† Is it not because of their natural humility that the poor are called the *temple* or *car* of the Schechina, of the Kingdom?‡ Is it not as a similar term that the Zohar first,§ and then the Ticounim ‖ call the Kingdom *humility?* Here doubtless are passages of great importance in the present question, and that seem to confirm all our conjectures.

But is this idea itself, apart from all cabalistic interpretation, unknown to Pharisaical Judaism? Is this partiality for the humble, is the special aptitude of these to become *chosen vessels* for all that concerns science, faith, and holiness, unknown to the Pharisees? Far from that; nothing comes so frequently to their lips. "With the humble God makes his Schechina rest."¶ Who is the true sage? said an ancient doctor; he who may be taught by all.** God's science is not in the heavens, said Moses; that is to say, add the doctors, thou shalt not find it in those whose pride reaches the sky.††
Where, on the contrary, shall one find it? in the lowly-minded, like water that comes from the mountains to sojourn in the valleys.‡‡
One is not ashamed, they say elsewhere, to ask even an inferior for water to slake thirst; so the great should not blush to ask the mean-

---

* Reschit Chokma, schaar haanava.   † Ibid.   ‡ Ibid, Chap. I.
§ Vol. III, page 280.   ‖ Reschit Chokma, ibid.   ¶ Sota.
** Aboth, IV.   †† Talmud, Treatise Eroubin, f. 55.   ‡‡ Taanit, page 7.

est for information as to **the law.*** **Of this** has not Juda the Holy, set us the most striking **example**? **Has he** not learned, as an humble disciple, his **own doctrines that he** had forgotten, from the mouth of a poor artisan?† Moreover, of **the** two rival doctrines of Hillel and Schammai, which one has definitely prevailed in Israel? That of the first, indeed, in consequence of his humility. He it is whom they propose as a model, saying : Be humble always like Hillel, and not overbearing like Schammai.‡ But what is of special importance to our subject, is that always and everywhere humility has been considered an indispensable requisite for the study of the formidable mysteries of the Mercaba, that is, as we think, of the doctrines that originated those of Jesus. From the most remote Talmudical times, to the Cabalists of the middle ages, all with one accord have required of the initiated perfect humility above all things.

We come now to the greatness of the humble, of *those who are at present the last, and who shall become the first, who humble themselves now and who shall be exalted.*§ Is not this a repetition of ancient Rabbinical doctrine? " What should a man do to win the love of mankind?" asks Alexander the Great of the doctors of the South (the Essenes, as we think). Let him hate dominion and authority, say the doctors. No, says Alexander, my maxim is better than yours; let him love them, that he may have the power to serve men.‖ Has not tradition preserved a favorite saying of the elder Hillel, long prior to Christianity: "My abasement shall be my elevation, and my elevation my abasement."¶ Is it not he who said : " He who grows proud shall perish."** Is not the following saying his master Abalion's ? " Flee grandeur."†† Has not one of the most ancient doctors said: " Be humble even to excess, for is not man's last hope the worms of his grave?"‡‡ Did not their disciples say: " Be lowly .... whoever humbles himself shall be exalted, and whoever exalts himself shall be humbled.§§ Whoever makes naught of himself here below for the Law's sake, shall be glorified hereafter."‖‖ To him who said he had seen in a dream the world reversed, that is to-say, the mountains down and the valleys up, did they not answer: " No, thou hast seen the actual world?"¶¶ And, in short, have they not summed the principle concisely thus : " Who is great is little, and who is little is great?"*** Moreover, what splendid promises are made them! What precious privileges are given them! They shall enjoy the Holy Spirit, as the old *Baraita* of R. Pinchas Ben Jair teaches, with whom humility holds the first rank of all virtues.

---

* Taanit, I. † Nedarim, IV. ‡ Eroubin, xlii.
‖ Marc. X, 31, &c. ‖ Talmud, Tamid. ¶ Vayicra, Rabba, sect. 81.
** Aboth, Chap. 1. †† Ibid. ‡‡ Ibid, Chap. IV.
§§ Talmud, Eroubin, fol. 13. ‖‖ Talmud, Berach, IX. ¶¶ Ibid, Pesahim, fol. 50.
*** Zohar, sect. Schelach-leka.

"The world to come," reply the doctors of Palestine to those of Babylon, "belongs to those who bend their knees, to the humble, the submissive, to those who meditate constantly and without being vain.* Their sins shall be forgiven who esteem themselves as abortions, as vile refuse."† If the fear of God is the crown of sages, it is but the shoe of the humble;‡ their prayer shall be granted, as they deem themselves but miserable flesh."§ And finally, " God himself shall be their crown."‖ Was anything stronger ever heard from the lips of Jesus or his apostles?

Here a question very interesting and, in more than one way, applicable to our subject, presents itself. What is the Gospel idea as to sovereign authority? Doubtless, in the midst of paganism, that, in practice at least, recognized no right but that of force, worshiped divine right enthroned, and thought sovereignty the privilege of birth, skill, or fortune only, the Gospel first proclaimed this great, fruitful idea that authority is nothing but a charge, an office, a servitude. In the Gospel we feel the new doctrine attacking, in close conflict, the old, and driving it to its furthest intrenchments. *Ye know*, said Jesus to his disciples, *that the princes of the Gentiles exercise dominion over them, and they that are great exercise authority upon them. But it shall not be so among you; but whosoever will be great among you, let him be your minister; and whosoever will be chief among you, let him be your servant.* A right which, though long a mere theory, failed not to temper occasionally, from the height of the Christian tribunal, the rigors of despotism, that the apathy of Christianity as to social life, had permitted to the thrones of Europe. Has Judaism ever taught anything else? Was the king ever other than the first subject of the law, the *ruler*, in the sense of the old Roman republic? Was royalty, according to the great definition of the doctors, aught else than servitude?¶ Was not David himself, that elect of God, quite legally degraded to the rank of simple citizen, when his popularity waned, and the sympathies of all were on Absalom's side? Is it not true, what the doctors say, that all human grandeur is bestowed only for the weal of Israel?** But Jesus, it will be said, points the remark: "For," said he, "even the son of man has not come to be served, but to serve." And when at table with his disciples: "I am in the midst of you, as one who serves." Now, is not this still pure Pharisaism; for here, too, God (whose character Jesus here assumes) is presented under the humblest forms, rendering personally to Israel in the desert, all the services that Abraham had rendered to the

---

* Talmud. Sanhed. † Ibid, Rosch, hasch, fol. 17. ‡ Midrasch, hazita.
§ Talmud. Sota, fol. 5. ‖ Ibid Meghilla. ¶ Talmud. Heroyoth. fol. 10.
** Talm. Berach, fol. 32.

angels in the valley of Mambre? And this is not the only instance (as we might show were it the place) of a reproduction, in Jesus' intercourse with his disciples, of the striking characteristics of ancient Jewish history.

Nothing is more closely allied to humility than *long-suffering*, and nothing, moreover, seems to be more the specialty of the gospel ethics. Is this, indeed, its parent? Has not this ethics found in Judaism maxims already made, of a character far superior, of a date far older? The famous precept, to offer the other cheek when smitten, had been long before suggested by his country's sufferings to Jeremiah, and criticism has already noticed it. Is Solomon's precept less precious? *Be thy heart*, he said, *insensible to what may be said against thee, even though thou shouldst hear thy slave curse thee*.* We shall not multiply citations from the Bible; as the Pharisees are on trial, they are the persons accused of being inferior to Jesus; these therefore we should ask for an account of their ethics. *The world*, they say, *is held together only by the merit of those who close the mouth when disputations arise*.† And to sum all in one fine sentence: *They who bear injury without returning it, they who hear themselves slandered and retort not, whose only impulse is love, who welcome with joy the evils of life, for them is it written in the prophets: The friends of God shall shine like the sun in his glory.* ‡

Let us here briefly examine a few other "beatitudes" related to the virtue of which we treat. *Happy are they who weep*, said Jesus, "*for they shall be comforted*. Pharisaism also had said: "Whoever mourns for Jerusalem shall share its future joy."§ "The tears of the distressed reach easily the throne of God."‖ "They are the greatest help, the most necessary condition to every prayer."¶ And what is noticeable is that the acknowledged chief of the Cabalistic school, R. Simeon Ben Jochai, is the author of the following maxim: *Man is not allowed to laugh unrestrainedly in this world*. Jesus continues (Mat. v. 7): *Blessed are the merciful for they shall obtain mercy*. And the Pharisees: "*Whoever shows mercy shall get it from God*;"** or again, in a more general way: "*As you measure, so shall it be meted unto you*;"†† and under this same form we meet the same thought in the Gospels. We read also: "*Happy are the peace-makers, for they shall be called children of God*." And this virtue is set down by the Pharisees among those that will be rewarded in this life and in the next;‡‡ Aaron's distinctive trait was that he reconciled brethren; this is the virtue that Hillel the Elder recommended, saying: "Be a

---

* Eccles, vii. 21.   † Talmud, Houllin, fol. 89.   ‡ Ibid, Schab, fol. 88, &c.
§ Ibid, Taanith, fol. 30.   ‖ Ibid, Baba metsia, fol 59.   ¶ Treat, Berachot, fol. 30.
** Talmud.   †† Ibid, Sota, fol. 8 and pass.   ‡‡ Mischna, treat, Peah., Chap, I.

follower of Aaron, loving peace, and seeking it everywhere, loving men and bringing them to the Law."*

Not all yet: *Happy,* says Jesus, *are they who are persecuted for Justice' sake, for theirs is the kingdom of heaven.*—Wouldst thou know, say the Pharisees, *how much God loves the persecuted? See the animals he chooses for sacrifice. Are there any more persecuted than the sheep, the pigeon, and the dove? Now God just prefers these to all other animals.*

But we must not conceal that the Pharisaical ethics not only rivals that of the Gospels, but transcends it when needed. Jesus exclaims: "*Happy those persecuted for the sake of righteousness* ;" that is, doubtless, those persecuted in the wrong, against all justice. But how, if the persecuted are guilty? No one knows. As to the Pharisees, their mercy knows no bounds, their charity is of a shade so delicate, of a tenderness so fine, that misery makes them forget all. They say, with Solomon : *God is found on the side of the persecuted. Is it only,* they add, *when the oppressed and the oppressors are equally just or impious? Is it only when the oppressor is an unjust man and the oppressed a just one? No; though the oppressor were just and the oppressed unjust, God is ever on the side of the latter.*†

An ethics that attains such hights has no rival to fear. Like Moses, who, according to the doctors, strove with the angels, it touches the very throne of God.

If there be a vice opposed to humility, it is pride and anger. Though the Gospel condemns both by implication in its exhortations to humility and meekness, it is very far from reaching that vehemence of condemnation which the Pharisees incessantly pour upon them. And we shall still be told, that those against whose pride and inordinate vanity Jesus thought proper to inveigh, were the holy doctors of Israel ! See the proud ! they say, "they deserve to be uprooted like idolatrous groves. Their dust shall not rise on the resurrection morn.‡ Though they should have reconciled heaven and earth with God (as did Abraham), they could not escape the pains of hell."§ "Let them be to you as idolators, atheists, or the incestuous. The Scheehina laments for them ; they and I—it says—cannot live together in the world."∥

As to the horror, in fact, with which the Pharisees regarded pride, we could cite examples without end. One, I hope, will suffice to show with what sort of pride the Gospels reproach the Pharisees. Rabbi Simeon, son of Gamliel, and Rabbi Ismael, the high priest, were led to martyrdom. The former began to weep. "Simeon, my brother, why weepest thou?" asked his companion ; "two steps more, and thou wilt be in heaven, beside thy fathers." "Why

*Aboth, Chap. III. †Vayikra Rabba, Chap. 27. ‡Sota, Chap. I. §Ibid. ∥Ibid.

should I not weep, **answered the** other, "when I share the lot of idolators, incestuous **people, homicides,** and breakers of the Sabbath?" "Has **it never** happened," replied the Rabbi, "that some one came **to consult thee** on a case **of conscience, and** that thy servants, **seeing thee** at table or in bed, sent **him away?**" "No," replied **the** other, "they had orders never to repel any one, whatever the **time** or circumstance. But God is just: **once** I was seated at **my** tribunal and the parties were standing waiting my judgment. **I** showed on that occasion pride, and God punishes me to-day."

And does the passionate man fare better? Already, before Jesus, had the Bible condemned him; the most **ancient** doctors had **said:** "Be not given to wrath."* They refined **soon** upon the old maxims: "Whoever," they tell us, "abandons himself to anger, has no respect for the Schechina itself."† "If the passionate man be a prophet his inspiration leaves him; **if a** doctor, he forgets his learning."‡ Who would **believe it**? The Pharisees, all submissive as they were to the **authority of** the Prophets, hesitated not to write these words: "**Why was** Elias snatched so soon from the earth? Because **he** gave **way to** anger and caused Baal's prophets to be slain. Then God took him from the world, saying: 'The earth needs not men like thee.'"§ Jesus condemns only causeless anger (Mat. **v.** 22); the Pharisees condemn it even when reasonable.

There is a sentence in the Gospels connected with our present subject. Sending his twelve disciples to preach to the Jews, Jesus **cautions them:** *Be ye wise as serpents and innocent as* ***doves****.* Does this idea, which is not ignoble and lacks not finesse if only for the antithesis, belong exclusively to Jesus and the Gospels? The Pharisees find its elements in the Bible. In one place they see Israel compared to the bravest and fiercest carnivora, **to** the lion, the wolf, and especially the serpent; in another it is **to a** dove God likens his Church. Whence this contradiction? "Ah"! say the doctors; "Israel is strong as a lion, wise as a serpent, but also innocent as a dove: strong and prudent with wolves into whose midst he is sent, to keep their strength at bay, to thwart their crafty schemes; but, innocent as the dove that gives **its** neck to death, Israel goes joyfully to martyrdom for his God and his faith."∥

Another **of** Jesus' favorite symbols is the child. David, many ages before, had said: "O Eternal, my heart is not haughty, nor mine eyes lofty, neither do I exercise myself in things too high for me, but I have considered my soul as a child in its mother's arms." (Ps. 131) The doctors went further still. They placed the figure

---

* Abath, Chap. II.   † Talmud, Nedarim.   ‡ Ib. Pesachim. f. 66.
§ Talmud, Schabbath, Chap. II.   ∥ Midrasch, treat. Schabb. f. 119.

of a child in the holy Mercaba, beside the Cherubs of Ezekiel. They taught that the world has no better stay than the pure breath of children;* comparing this breath with that of the holiest Pharisees, they say: "Far different is the breath that finds the taste of sin (that of the Pharisees) from that (the child's) which finds it not."† They represent God as a tender father pleased at their childish studies, at their first stammerings in the holy Law; they esteemed their minds the sharpest for heavenly things, and gave them priority as to the revelations about the Red Sea and Sinai, where, they say, the child, seated on its mother's knees, was the first to raise its head, to recognize the Eternal, and to utter these words of the Canticle: *There is my God,* "Wouldst thou know how much children are loved by God? When Jerusalem was destroyed by the Babylonians, the representatives of all Israel (who were there for the sacrifices), went away, but the Schechina still remained. The Sanhedrim broken up, the Schechina still rested within its walls; but when the children were carried away prisoners, then the Schechina went with them, for it is written: 'Thy children have walked captives before the enemy; then departed from Sion all its glory'" (Lam. I, 5–6). And to sum all, the doctors arranged for the Synagogue prayers, wherein, with the merits of Abraham, Isaac, and Jacob are invoked those of innocent childhood. But what is at once the type and the explanation of Jesus' partiality for children, is this remarkable statement from the Zohar: *Little children who die young are taught in Paradise by the Messiah himself.*

Another kindred virtue is *truth*, which Jesus seems to recommend by condemning duplicity and **hypocrisy**. Is this a virtue unknown to the Pharisees? Truth! which, with *justice* and *peace*, as says an ancient doctor, makes one of the three pillars of society.‡ *The seal of God is truth;*§ a sublime saying that lifts us to Plato. Who shall not see God's face? First, hypocrites, then liars. Imitate, rather, Rab Safra. An article of his was being sold; a higher price was constantly offered, since the doctor, who was praying, would not stop to reply. When done, he said to the buyer, "My friend, take it at such a price (a lower one), since at that I resolved to sell it." For such a man, say the doctors,‖ has David said, "O God, who shall be worthy to dwell in thy tabernacle, upon thy holy mountain? He who speaks the truth *in his heart*." Is it a virtue less needful to the Pharisees? Hear then: "Let man be ever submissive to God's will, in private as well as in public" (repeated, from a very old text, every day by the Israelite). "The doctor, whose interior is not as his exterior, deserves not the title, doctor."¶ He should be cast

---

* Talmud, treat. Schabb, f. 119.   † Talmud, trait. Schabb, f. 119.   ‡ Aboth, Chap. I.
§ Yoma, fol. 69, &c.   ‖ Talmud, Baba Bathr., f. 88, &c.   ¶ Yoma, f. 72.

to the dogs.* Let him beware of all lying, even of telling a child, "I shall give thee something," if he means not to give; for he would lie and teach the child to lie.† Is more wanted? We meet nothing till we reach the simile by which Jesus expresses the hypocrisy of the pseudo-Pharisees, viz., *whitened sepulchres*. This is found in the oldest Pharisaism, and, moreover, is applied, just as Jesus applies it, to false Pharisees. Gamliel (the same, perhaps, who taught Saul) having withheld the right of entrance to the academy from every Pharisee whose sincerity was not well known, *whose inside was not as his outside* (in the words of the Rabbies), reproved himself for his severity, saying, "Alas! perhaps I have deprived some noble soul, hidden in the mass, of the word of God." To calm his scruples, he was shown, in a dream, *whitened barrels full of ashes*, and a voice said to him: " These are the Pharisees whom thou hast repelled."

The love of truth brings us to self-denial, one of those virtues most recommended in the Gospels. *He*, we are told (John, XII, 25), *who loves his own life shall lose it; but he who despises it shall find it in life eternal*; and Paul to the Romans (VIII, 13): "If ye live after the flesh ye shall die; but if ye mortify the lusts of the flesh through the spirit ye shall live." Could both be ignorant of a tradition current in Judea from Alexander's time? The son of Philip was not above putting some questions to the doctors of the South (very probably the Essenes), and among others the following: "What should man do to live? Let him die. And what should he do to die? Let him live, they replied."‡ Where shall you find the Law? In him who fears not, for its sake, utter privation,§ who hesitates not to be esteemed a fool,‖ and to sacrifice for it life itself.¶ "He who is worthy of being my follower," said Jesus, " must brave all suffering." " Whosoever takes not up his cross to follow me, is not worthy of me." It is from Pharisaism, evidently, that he takes this language, while, however, supplanting the *Law, truth, justice, God* (alone worthy, according to the doctors, of every sacrifice), by his personality, by the *I* of Jesus.[1] *The carrying of his cross*, scarcely reaches the idea of the *cross*, that his masters, the Pharisees, long

* Talmud. † Succa, f. 46. ‡ Talmud, tr. Tamid, Chap. IV.
§ Sota, Chapter 2. ‖ Ibid. ¶ Talmud, Berach, 63, &c.
** Ibid. Trait. Berachot, fol. 5.

[1.] And truly, whatever he lacked of self-glorification and self-sufficiency, his followers, putting him in the very stead of God and calling him (Rev. XII, 13) the *Alpha and Omega*, (a phrase applicable exclusively to the Deity, see Isa, XLIV, 6), have amply supplied. Whether or not such an arrogation be a breach of the first Commandment, a consideration of Isaiah, Chapter 42, 8, "I am the Lord, that is my name; and my glory will I not give to another;" and, 43, 10th and 11th verse, "*and besides Me there is no Savior*," may help Christians to decide.—[*Trans*.

before expressed. Who, for them, is Isaac carrying the wood for his own pyre? He is the man bearing the cross. Is there aught in this world finer, dearer, more sacred than country, than the Law (*Thora*), than Heaven (*Olam habba*)? Well! neither Law, country, nor heavenly bliss can be gained without grief, suffering and self-denial.** And who is the author of this great truth! *Rabbi Simeon Ben Jochai*, the man whose teachings have inspired all Christianity, its dogmas as well as its ethics. And what commentary on this law of self-denial more quick than the history of Judaism! God "shows his goodness even to the thousandth generation of those who love him," says Moses. Who loves him, adds the Mekhilta, better than Israel, who died a thousand times for him? Why art thou led to the scaffold?—Because I circumcised my child. Why art thou nailed to the cross?—Because I have obeyed the commands of the Most high. Why art thou whipped?—Because I have taken up the loulab (palm-branch)

In vain does Christian ethics, as if to defy the ancient ethics of Israel, raise the standard of its requirements; it finds the latter always beyond it. To the rich man, who asks to follow him, Jesus says: "Go sell all thou hast and give to the poor; it is harder for a rich man to enter the kingdom of heaven than for a camel to pass through the eye of a needle." We do not here investigate the effect of this condemnation of wealth upon social life. We know that when Christianity saw not the era of the resurrection dawning as quickly as it expected, when, with good grace or with bad, it found itself engaged in our actual life, with its needs, demands, and future, it took care to distinguish *counsel* from precept, and simply recommended voluntary poverty. If we were examining this aspect of the question, we should remark that so absolute a judgment from Jesus against the rich and riches, that the constant and general practice in the primitive church of each one's selling his property and laying it at the feet of the apostles (as in the terrible example of Ananias and Saphira), do not permit us to make any sort of distinction. If we are deeply convinced of anything it is that, as Jesus pretended to make the highest and most exceptional Pharisaical doctrines common property, so he pretended to impose on mankind those exceptional virtues, those heroic acts, that ascetic morality, that absolute self-detachment of which the greatest Pharisees often gave examples; in short, to bestow upon the Pagan masses the theology and ethics of the Mystics, and to stifle the world in an Essenic cloister

These examples, however, exist. Useless to name the Rekabites who, from the time of Jeremiah, at the command of the prophet, renounced the holding of personal property; or the Essenes (whose connection with **the former is nearer than** is supposed) who imitated them **in this point as in others** still. But how pass over the examples furnished **us by the** history of the **Pharisees?** Monobaza, King **of Adiabene,** brought up in Pharisaism, **though** keeping his throne, **learned** doubtless from this school to give **alms** royally ; in years of famine he opened the royal wealth to all his subjects, and the **remarks** of courtiers only brought upon them that noble response to **which,** when speaking of charity, we shall soon revert. Could **we,** without injustice, suppress names as ancient as venerable ? Was **it** from the Gospels that the ancient doctor Eleazar of Bartotha learned **to** give his substance to the poor, to such a degree that the almoners carefully avoided him, lest they should deprive him of his scant daily earnings ? Was **it** from **Jesus,** whom he long preceded, that Hillel learned to divide **men into four** classes according to each's love **of** riches, and to **rank him who** said, "Mine is thine, even as is thine own," with **Hasid, a name, as we** think, indicative **of** the Essenes ? Was **R. Isbab, who gave** his blood for his country and all his goods to the **poor, taught by** Christianity ? Was that Rabbi Johanan a Christian, **who,** walking with his disciples between Tiberias and Sipporis, pointed now to a cornfield, now to an olive grove, now to a vineyard, saying, *I have sold all to devote myself to the study of the Law;* and who said, smiling, to his disciple Hiya Bar Abba (who wept because he had "reserved nothing for his old age"): **" My son** Hiya, thinkest thou not that I have made a good bargain ? **I have e**xchanged things that were made in six days for those that **took forty** days and as many nights?" The text adds : " When Rabbi **Johanan** died, his cotemporaries applied to him this verse of the Canticle: *Man gives all for love; Rabbi Johanan gave all for the Law.*

Are these but rare examples? What we have **said** elsewhere **of** the Essenes forbids us to think so. But the **moral** contagion that had seized the Jewish **masses,** the renunciation **of** all wealth, **voluntary** poverty, this *communism of love,* went, it seems, so far in **Palestine,** that a law had to interpose. The practical sense, sociability, **and** moderation of the Judaic spirit soon set the law (that idol **of the** Jews) between **generosity** and self-spoilation. And this **protective law** was **enacted at** Ouscha where the doctors, meeting **to put a stop to** this barren frittering of the **public** wealth, decreed **that it was** unlawful for any one to give in alms more than a *fifth* of his property ; **an** enormous figure, and one which well attests the force and demands of that public spirit to **which** the doctors dared **not** concede less than a *fifth,* so irresistible in Israel was the impulse **to** Charity !

CHAPTER VI

CHARITY.

ACCUSATIONS OF JESUS.—THEY STRIKE AT THE BIBLE AS WELL AS AT THE PHARISEES.— CIVIL LAW AND MORAL LAW; NECESSITY OF DISTINGUISHING.— CUPIDITY AND ANGER CONDEMNED BY THE PHARISEES.—THEIR EXPANSION OF THE DECALOGUE. SUPPOSED SUPERIORITY OF GOSPEL CHARITY.—GOD IS CHARITY.—HEBREW CHARITY; DISTINCT FROM ALMS WHICH IT EXCLUDES.—THE THREE ENEMIES.—WHO THE ENEMY ACCORDING TO THE GOSPEL.—COUNTRY AND SOCIETY IN CHRISTIANITY.— PARABLE OF THE SAMARITAN.

We have written the word *charity*. If there be any pretention dating from the founder of Christianity, it is unquestionably that of having supplanted the Law, the faith of Israel, by charity. One has but to glance at the fifth chapter of Matthew to see this pretention to superiority, so lauded since. It is curious to see how the emphasized protestations of Jesus against a desire to abolish the Law blend with his assumption of superiority to it; a tendency not to be denied, and one which he hides with difficulty under the idea of a moral progress. "Think not I am come to destroy the Law or the prophets; I am come not to destroy, but to fulfill them" (verse 17). He explains this in detail in verse 21: "Ye have heard that it was said by them of old time, thou shalt not kill . . . &c; but I say unto you, that whosoever is angry with his brother without a cause shall be in danger of the judgment; and whoever shall say to his brother, Raca, (wicked one) shall be in danger of the council; but whosoever shall say, thou fool, shall be in danger of hell fire." And further on (verses 27 and 28): "Ye have heard that it was said by them of old time, thou shalt not commit adultery; but I say unto you, &c." It is this perpetual opposition, established by Jesus, between the requirements of the Old Law and those of the new Covenant, that we are about to examine. Is not the design of this Law to protect the life, the character, or the property of man in the social state? And would not an injury to them be a flagrant violation of the simplest duties of charity? Ought we not see if Judaism be really guilty of so grave omissions, before asking it how it has provided for the performance of the *positive* duties of charity? Should not accusations be rebutted before preferring one's claims to the gratitude of mankind? We are sorry to say that these charges could not be more formally made than in the words of Jesus; Judaism could not be more directly accused, or its honor more assailed. Is it only tradition and the Pharisees that are struck at? Impossible; the 20th verse, that seems to warrant this doubt, is but a bait for the ignorant. The idea of **progress, and** consequently of imperfection, about which we **have spoken,** above **all** those solemn words, "You have heard **what they said in old** time," exclude the supposition of the Pharisees **merely ; and the** Bible **texts** themselves, cited as proof of imperfection, **cap the** impossibility of a construction **that** sometimes **seems** favorable for a Christian apology. **It is** then, beyond doubt, **that** the Bible, Moses, God himself are arraigned, and we **might be** tempted to let Christian ethics kill itself by that surcharge **of** vanity which mines beneath itself a pit, **wherein** its own titles **and very** foundation can forever disappear. The imputation is, however, **so** bold and so opposed to the plainest facts, that it will not be without use in this long-vexed question **to** see how they have managed to foist upon the world notions that, **even to-day,** are not **quite** dissipated.

As we **have said before, we must, if we would avoid error,** carefully distinguish between **two things in** Judaism. **There is** the civil law, that shields the **life, honor,** and property **of the** citizen, and **whose** administration **is** confined **to** the Courts. And there is the **moral law, the duties** whereof, a thousand times recalled in the Bible, **are naturally set** forth **in tradition and** in the teachings of the doctors. A double law corresponding to the two-fold character **of the** Jews, **to their** polity and to their religion. The one is best represented by the Mosaic code, the other by the prophets first and by **the** doctors afterwards. Would it be right to judge of Jewish ethics by **the** law of Moses? As well expect to find French mo**rality in the** *Code civil,* or English morality in the *Magna Charta!* **No** conclusion, then, could be come to against Judaism **as** long as **we limited** ourselves solely to the Mosaic code.

But even **within those** just limits, **can we say that** Jesus is right ? **Is** the superiority of his ethics to the **Mosaic Law** well established ? **No.** If there be any point where these two constituents of Israelitic life, *Justice* and *Charity* intersect, where the character of **the** former is more closely moulded to that **of** the latter, **where, in** short, the law is eminently *charitable,* it is precisely, we must **say,** where Jesus selects the battle-ground for the two contending **systems.** Assuredly he **could have made** no worse choice. Let **us see.**

Matt. **V: 25 :—"Ye have** heard what **was said by them** of old time : thou **shalt** not commit adultery ; *but I say **unto** you* whosoever looketh on **a** woman to lust after her, hath committed adultery **with** her already **in** his heart." Now, we need not search far to find **in the** decalogue itself, the Tenth Commandment interdicting the desire spoken of by **Jesus. Was it calumny, or** forgetfulness on his part ? We think, **neither. The key to the enigma is,** we think, this: Tradition, while preserving the full force of the said commandment, while giving the widest and most absolute interpretation to that of Deuteronomy, subjected, however, that of Exodus (expressed differently) to one condition (so that the violator could be prosecuted, which for a mere desire or intention could not have been done), namely: to **that of actual commission**. Then and then only could the civil law **interpose**; then only could there be adultery, and not after a mere desire, as Jesus asserts. This is the strange abuse which the Gospel makes of the Pharisaical exposition. Far from abating the severity of the Mosaic Code, the doctors only regulated the action of the Courts, established impassable limits for human laws by carefully distinguishing what is cognizable by the *interior Court*, where God alone presides, from the overt act cognizable by the magistrate. Have they subtracted, thereby, aught from the weight of the precept of Deuteronomy, where the verbage assumes, to their view, quite a different latitude? In no wise; and the proof is the rigor of their own morals as to all kinds of impudicity. To look on a woman with lust, to look at one of her fingers even, her hair, to listen to her song, &c., all this was for the Pharisees not indeed adultery, but grave sin; which still gives but a faint idea of their austerity in this respect. What precept can be more severe than this: *If thy right eye make a slip, tear it out and cast it from thee; for it is better that one of thy members perish than that thy whole body be cast into hell.* Well, before this precept was even written, before Origen's strange application of it, Judaism venerated the chief Pharisee at Rome, the hero Rabbi Mathia Ben Haras, who, tormented by temptation, tore his eyes out, to be rid of it.

Were there no other proofs, Jesus himself could give us some. For the worst accusation that Pharisaism could imagine against its formidable foe, was that he one day said of some lovely Madeline, "What fine eyes that girl has."* When one sees in this a grave fault, a crime, one is far from a moral laxity. One remark still remains as to the term *adultery* which Jesus gives to a mere desire. What we are about to read will prove that, forgetting the civil character of the Mosaic code, he not only charges this code with the crime of neglecting to legislate for ethics, but, by a deplorable confusion of ideas, he substitutes ethics and intention or desire for the Law and the overt act, giving them the gravity and even the penal obligation of the latter, just as, on the other hand, he absolves the actual adulteress by a mere word; a double and grave abuse which Jesus' successors but too well perpetuated.

* Talmud Sanhed, f. 107.

Thus (Mat. **V, 21, 22**) he says : " **Ye have heard that** it was said by them of old **time, thou shalt not kill; and** whosoever shall kill shall be in **danger of the** judgment; *but I say unto you that whosoever is angry with his brother without a cause* **shall be** *in danger of the judgment; and whosoever shall say to his brother Raca shall be punished by* **the Council,** *but whosoever shall say thou fool,* **shall be** *punished by hell-fire.*" Before examining the injustice of this, let us **see what** it has **too much** or too little. *Causeless* anger is **forbidden; and** should provoked anger be not so too? Pharisaical morality **avoids** well **this** restriction—that would allow every one to justify his anger—by forbidding *all anger*. But what is there too much in the sentence of Jesus? Clearly **a** disregard of the most natural distinction (one that Judaism never **omits to** make) **between** *justice* and *charity*, between *the civil code* and *the ethics*. Jesus **will not have it.** He sends the passionate man **to** *the judgment*, **just as he does the** homicide in the preceding **verse. The man who says** *Raca* **to** his brother, shall be *punished by the Council*. **Where is the code that** would sanction such enormities? **Where is the law that would prosecute** anger or cite to **its bar him who** should **call any one a fool** or empty-head (Raca)? **And is** this the fault in **the law of** Moses? **In** truth, it should be proved that it provided not against such dispositions. But it is not alone the excess, but also the confusion of punishments for **which** the verse is remarkable. *Prison* **and** *hell* are there thrown pell-mell from a hand that seems in haste to punish, **to** refine on **the old** Mosaic justice, rather than guided **by prudence or** justice. **For anger and** the epithet raca, the civil **courts; for the** epithet fool, **hell-fire. What** confusion, what **a jumbling of** religion and the penal code, of demons and policemen, **of hell and prison?** And the last jumble already marks the future **and is the first** step to the auto-da-fes, to the **dungeons** of the Inquisition. In short, Jesus, **as** far as sending to **hell the** man who calls **his** neighbor a fool is concerned, is not mistaken **as to** jurisdiction. But having come **to this,** what we should examine **is, if** Judaism, making the proper **distinction between the civil code and** the ethical, has anything **to learn,** to envy in an ethics **that wants, at** any price, to be thought *new*. We think not. Doubtless **the Mosaic** code could not legislate against evils of a purely spiritual character. Moral derelictions are so well condemned **by** the examples of our great men, by general precepts **to** love, charity, justice, &c., that one could **not accept or** love the Bible without hating all kinds of vice or passion. **But we should seek** in vain **for** special condemnations of them; for the Pentateuch is, **as we have said, but** (chiefly) a civil code, while ethics is the concern of tradition and **the doctors. And is** this last, taken in its own proper **sphere,** less pure **and elevated than** that of the Gospels? **Are** moral vices and faults less severely condemned there than in the Gospels? But there are none of those minutiæ, of those refinements on ethics wherein the Gospel affects pre-eminence, of which the types and origins may not be found in the old Pharisaical morality. Needless to say that the term *impious* given to a man, is sufficient cause for citation before the Council ;* that the mere lifting of one's hand against another, without striking, is called impiety, and is punishable by the courts ;† that anger is, on one side, compared to *suicide*,‡ for, as says the Talmud, it is of the passionate man that the prophet has said: "Depart from him who wounds himself by anger," and that, on the other side, it is ranked with homicide (not always cognizable by the Courts), if it is carried so far as to make its object blush, so that, as say the doctors, "the white and red alternate on his face,"§ even though the reproaches had reference to the guilt of some great crime. But what is truly remarkable, and what wrests from the hands of Christian ethics the scepter it has usurped, is that, of all enormous crimes, the only ones that form an exception to the great Jewish principle of *non-eternity of punishment*, are three against morality, and the first two are the objects of these evangelical imprecations. "Though one were the greatest sinner in the world," say the Pharisees, "hell cannot hold him forever ; all shall one day see the light of Heaven and Paradise." Do you know who shall never see it? He who calls his neighbor a *bad* name, he who makes his neighbor blush by scandalous proposals, and the adulterer. This is the ethics of those formulistic Pharisees, those adorers of the letter, of those heartless men whom the Gospel paints for us. This is the mould from which the Gospel ethics copied the *raca*, the *fool*, sent by it to the galleys or hell's-fire. Is this all? No ; Pharisaical ethics is so refined, so delicate, has such exquisite shades that no rival whatever could be found for it. "Better that a man throw himself into a burning furnace than make his fellow-man blush before the world."‖ And who is the author of this saying? He who is the best representative of the school from which Christianity, as we have reiterated, has drawn its dogmas and ethics—Rabbi Simeon Ben Jochai. "Whosoever shall make his brother blush, shall himself blush when the angels repel him from the mansion of the Most High.¶" The most precious benediction which the Pharisees gave their disciples was : "God be thanked that thou never hadst reason to blush or madest another do so."** And an old rabbinical text, says : "He who profanes holy things, who despises solemnities, who annuls the covenant of Abraham, our

---

* Talmud.   † Ibid.   ‡ Talmud and Zohar, sct. Tetzave.   § Talmud, Baba, Metzia, f. 58.
‖ Ib., Sota, fol. 10.   ¶ Massechet, Kalla.   ** Moed Katan, f. 9.

father, who gives a false sense **to the law,** *who makes his neighbor blush* (literally, **grow pale**) **in public, shall** have *no part in the world to come.* Not from **Jesus but** from the Pharisees comes this.

There **are** several other points in which Jesus attempts to establish the superiority of his code to the old. Though our preceding remarks are no less applicable to the whole tenor of his teaching, we shall not examine the latter at this moment, as not bearing directly upon charity. The laws of divorce, oaths, and retaliation must then wait their turn; but we would now compare the ideas **of** the old law with those of the new respecting *the love of one's neighbor.*

We would first ask, why does Jesus—taking the second part of the Decalogue in his comparisons as to homicide, adultery, false swearing—omit to mention theft, commercial deceit? In this case, as he has done in the others, he could have refined upon the legal enactments of the Pentateuch, and gained the easy victory that even the poorest moralist can, over the dry prescriptions of the civil and criminal code. Perhaps he saw tradition lifting itself with full force to supply amply the needs of the strict Mosaic law. However that be, we ought to show the reader the wonderful expansion, or rather fecundation effected by tradition upon the law of Moses. We must see what those dry, bare formulas, *steal not, cheat not,* become under the breath of tradition, as we have had a specimen in the two commandments—thou shalt not kill, and thou shalt not commit adultery.

In the eye of tradition, he who gains the public favor by feigned virtue, by imposture, is a thief. To press your hospitality on any one without seriously meaning to give it, to make great offers, knowing that they will not be accepted, is always, as the ancient Tossifta declares, to steal in some fashion. Would it be more excusable, perchance, in the sight of the Eternal? Error to think so. "Whosoever steals the esteem, the good opinion of his creatures, steals the esteem of the Most High;" to take advantage of an ambiguity, to get a credit one does not deserve, is just simply **to** steal. "If thou hast a torn garment, take care not to head a funeral procession; for it may be thought you share in the grief of relatives and friends; it would be to steal both from the living and the dead." (Moed Kathan, 26). Shouldst thou leave the town to take the air, take care not to accept the thanks of any visiting friend who supposes that thou wast going to meet him. Otherwise thou wilt be far from following the example of Rab Safra, who, in such a case, hastened to undeceive his friend by telling him that he knew not at all of his arrival. Dost thou think **that this strict sincerity is** imposed on thee with reference to thy co-religionists **only**? The Pharisee, Samuel, the physician of Juda the Holy, the friend of Plotinus, is at hand to undeceive thee. He requires the greatest sincerity in our dealings with all men, whether Jews or Gentiles, and he is the first to illustrate personally that we cannot, without sin, act otherwise; as witness the anecdote wherein Samuel reproaches his servant for having offered a boatman a mixture of wine and water, as pure wine. So much as to theft.

And as to deceit—to take advantage of your brother's mean or Pagan origin, of his dishonorable past, or unfortunate present, to say to him, remember your past life, your ancestors; your mouth that now utters the truth and the praise of the Everlasting, was formerly polluted with blood, strangled meats, impure food; your sufferings are but the just punishment of your former faults. "And which of the two is worse?" asks the great doctor of the Cabalistic school, R. Simeon Ben Jochai. "It is the former who is a hundred times more guilty. For does he not attack a man's honor, a thousand times more precious than money? Is it not a far more irreparable loss than the most flagrant fraud, which may at any time be repaired with money."

This sincerity, this perfect magnanimity, were so well rooted in the Jewish heart, that all the splendor of the tiara could not dazzle them, when that tiara was stained by such baseness as the foregoing. Thus the memory of a Pontiff, whose generosity equaled not his dignity, remained forever disgraced in Israel. He had just performed the majestic ceremonies of the Day of Atonement. Followed by the crowd, he was almost borne in triumph to their abode. Suddenly the crowd opened to let two men in foreign dress and of strange tongue, pass; they were proselytes! Schemaia and Abtalion, two masters venerated in Israel, the teachers of Hillel and Schammai. The indiscreet and proud Pontiff thus addressed them: *Let the sons of the Gentiles come in peace.* "Yes," replied the doctors, lowering their eyes, "let the sons of the Gentiles come in peace if they do the works of Aaron; but let not the sons of Aaron come in peace, if they have not also his virtues and his works."* And Israel has ever repeated: Let the sons of the Gentiles come in peace, if they practice the virtues of Aaron.

We see that the most indirect offence to Charity is most severely condemned by the Hebrew ethics. But is Charity itself there? There seems a doubt about the matter, so accustomed are people to make the terms Christianity and Charity synonymous. We repeat that there are subline traits of character in the Gospels. But

---

* Talmud, Yoma, f. 71.

is this to say that it **is there as a** *new precept*, as, to our great astonishment, the Gospel **declares?** It is perhaps unjust to say so even respecting **Paganism;** but it is absurd as regards Hebraism. In vain would **Christianity** lift itself into the regions of an almost mystical **morality**; it is on the wings of Hebraism that it **soars to** these heights. In vain does it assert "God is Charity,"—**this** sublime saying that deeply stirred the whole Pagan world lapped in sensuality—it got this from Judaism. "God is Charity, God is **Love**," **says the** Cabala, and also the Midrasch. **And** what have the doctors made of the Mosaic precept, "Love thy neighbor as thyself?" They have made it the great principle of **the** law, according to Akiba, or, according to Hillel, that, *of which the whole law is but the commentary.* They **have** changed the concluding words of the verse, *I am the Eternal*, **into an oath** of righteous justice against all who practiced not **this precept.** They have given *Charity* this comprehensive appellation, **Ghemilouth** *hassadim.* Now, **at** what do they **hold** this? **No ideas more noble** could **be** entertained. *It is, with Doctrine and* **Religion, one of** *the three* **pillars of the Universe.** *It is the beginning, middle, and end of the law;* **for this** last shows us at its commencement **God** giving man **a** companion; secondly, God visiting **Abraham;** and, finally, still God appointing **a tomb for** Moses. **Without** this, science, faith, worship, will never **make aught but a man** without God, without **that God of truth of whom it is written**: "Israel shall remain many **days without the God of truth.**"* (Hence the *practice of truth* spoken of by the Gospels.) **Without** this, possess what virtues he **may, a man** can be at best but *badly righteous;* he alone being **perfect who is** good **towards both** God and men, while the **other is so only towards** the **Lord. On the** other hand, with Charity, **all other** virtues go ; for Rabban Johanan Ben Zaccai having challenged **all** his disciples to **say** which virtue they thought the greatest, **and** Eleazar having said that it was a good **heart,** the **master said:** *I think the judgment of Eleazar better than* **yours,** *for all yours are contained in his.*† **Had Sodom** and its sisters **this, they would** have found mercy at **the bar** of the Eternal, idolatrous **and corrupt though** they were—had only the incense of a little Charity perfumed the rankness of **their** vices. Thanks to **this,** Micha, the idolatrous Jew, was tolerated a long time, though the angels accused **him** before God, **saying**: "See Lord, the smoke **from** thy altars mingles with that **of the** offerings to Micha's idol!" And God replied, "Leave **him in peace**; his bread is offered to **poor** travelers."‡ This is more than **all the** sacrifices in the world ; **more** than holocaust or sin-offering ; and consoles us

---

* Aboda Zara, from 10 Chron. xv. 3.   † Aboth, Chap. 2.   ‡ Talmud, tr. Sanhedr, 103.

in exile for the overthrow of temple and altar. It did so for an eye witness of his country's fall! Rabbi Johanan Ben Zakkai was walking one day through the streets of Jerusalem, and Rabbi Jehoschoua followed him. All at once they came upon the ruins of the temple. Rabbi Jehoschoua sighing, **said**: " Woe to us! Who henceforth shall atone for our sins?" "**Be comforted,** my son," said the master, " we **have** still **a substitute in** *Charity,* **for** it is written, ' I love Charity more than **sacrifice.**'"* **And after** the fall of the first temple, **did not** Daniel, **in** Babylon, **offer to God** Charity, in place of sacrifice, **by** rejoicing **at the** weddings of the **poor, by** burying the **dead, and** giving alms ;† in short, by this **is the true** Israelite recognized. Whoever possess the three following **virtues** are of the lineage of our father Abraham ; who lack them, **are not** his children ; his true children are compassionate, modest, and **charitable.** (Gomle chassodim.)†

Is this Charity alms ? **We** have seen how different it is from **this** ; and in that difference lies not the least noble trait of Pharisaical morality. Is it to be wondered at that primitive Christianity should have made so much of it, putting Charity above all special benevolence of which it is the soul and spring? Paul and Clement, of Alexandria, have, they too, well said : "Works, even for a good purpose, have no merit for salvation, except through Charity ; and this is the measure of their actual worth." But is not the Pharisaical doctrine taught in express terms **Not** only is Charity carefully distinguished from simple alms-giving, and from every other good work, but it is declared far superior to **all** special benevolence, to Tzedaka, for instance, which it surpasses, they add, in many respects ; for the one has to **do but** with things exterior to man ; the other, with man's whole nature, **body** and soul ; the one serves the living only ; **the other, the dead** as well ; the **one** concerns itself for the poor only ; the **other, for the** rich also ; **for with them,** too, Charity finds wounds **to heal, tears** to dry, **griefs to** ease.† And more: alms-giving itself is rewarded only *so far as it is transfused by* **Charity ;** for it is written, " Sow *alms,* **and** you can reap only according to *Charity."* (Hos. x, 12). And if he who gives his mite to the poor deserves six blessings, he who soothes an affliction, who gives not his bread but, (as the Doctors finely comment on the text) his *soul,* the latter shall have the eleven blessings named by the prophet Isaiah.§

This Charity, that doubtless found with the Pharisees its widest application, may be understood as having limits, as applying

---

* **Maghen** aboth, from Talmud, tr. Soucca, 49.   †Talmud Yebomath, 79.
‡ Massechet Kala.   § Baba Bathra.

to friends only, as **excluding** enemies, whether personal, religious, or political. Does Jewish Charity recognize this distinction? A delicate question as between Judaism and Christianity! Not observing the capital distinction between the Jewish State and the Jewish faith, but taking Hebraism as a homogeneous whole, some consider Hebrew Charity quite equal to the Christian, and some, far inferior. But, by observing the distinction, we can see wherein Hebrew Charity is similar to, diverse from, or superior to the other.

As regards the *personal enemy*, we must reserve for that a special consideration. What does Judaism teach as to the remaining two? By this classification we can better appreciate the merit Christianity decrees itself, and the airs it has put on from the evangelical era to the present time, on the score of its unlimited Charity. With respect to this comparison, Matthew (v, 43 and seq.) writes: " Ye have heard, adds Jesus, that it was said: *Thou shalt love thy neighbor and hate thine enemy; but I say unto you, love your enemies and bless those who curse you.*" By the words, *ye have heard*, Jesus doubtless refers to the Law of Moses. There is not, I dare say, one of the precepts named in this chapter, upon which an improvement is pretended, that does not belong to the Mosaic code. We are forced, then, to refer verse 43 to the Mosaic code, and must, for other reasons, consider it a textual citation from the Law, its form being different from the style of Jesus, whenever *the tradition of men* clashes (as he thinks) with the *word of God*. This being established, it is not easy to detect the origin and true meaning of this imputation, so expressly does it seem forged to give the new law pre-eminence, and so little root does it appear to have in either the text or spirit of the Scriptures. What first strikes us is, that while the preceding citations from the Pentateuch, in this chapter, are almost literal extracts from the text, in vain shall we search the whole five books to discover any verse that tallies, in either the letter or spirit, with that given us by Jesus. In Leviticus, indeed, we have the first half of the verse, *Thou shalt love thy neighbor* ; but where, in the name of wonder, shall we find the other half, *thou shalt hate thine enemy*? Can we doubt that Jesus has assigned to Hebrew Charity the limits that his imagination only and his prejudices suggested? That he has brought false, not to say malicious, suit against it? Before examining whether there be anything in the *spirit* of the Mosaic code to warrant this charge, let us turn to another Gospel text, which may throw light on our subject.

A Doctor of the Law, as Luke says (x, 25 and seq.), came to **Jesus**, and, in Pharisaical fashion, of which examples abound in the **Talmud**, asked him, *Master, what must I do to gain eternal life*? To which Jesus replied: "What is written in the Law?" and he said, *Thou shalt love the Lord, thy God, &c.,* . . *and thy neighbor as thyself.* To which Jesus replied, "Thou hast answered well; do this and thou shalt live." But, wishing to justify himself, the Doctor asks furthermore: "And who is my neighbor?" To which Jesus replies, "A certain man went down from Jerusalem to Jericho," &c. Nothing improbable in the Doctor's question, whether he asked it for the sake of instruction, or, as is more likely, to test Jesus. But scarcely have we taken the first step, when the probability of the occurrence diminishes and we cannot but suspect that we have to do merely with a dramatic scene, drawn by an awkward hand, for the purpose of displaying the superiority of Christian to Jewish ethics. The whole character of this narrative from Luke, and the passage from Matthew, lead us to the conclusion that Hebrew Charity stopped at a fixed point, *the enemy*, whether we understand this word in a general sense or in the special one intimated by the Samaritan of the Gospel parable.

But who, according to the Gospel itself, is this enemy? It is first, the personal enemy. Can we doubt it. The antitheses of *neighbor* and *enemy*, in Matthew (v, 43), of phrases such as these,— *Do good to those who hate you; pray for those who persecute you; for if you love only those who love you, &c.*—and the conclusion drawn from the parable of the Samaritan, all show that it is the *personal enemy* whom we must hate according to Judaism and love according to the Gospel. But the political enemy is no less clearly designated by the Samaritan of the parable. This enemy too, then, we must hate, according to one system, and love according to the other. But is this the actual teaching of Judaism? Are we to take this gross caricature for the true portrait of Hebrew ethics? Omitting, for the moment, what regards the *personal enemy*, our task is very simple here. We shall ask ourselves if the love of one's neighbor, commanded by the law of Moses, allows us to exclude the stranger, the non-Israelite; or if, indeed, within the limits necessary to political existence, the Charity of Israel knows no bounds, but, like that of God himself, includes all mankind.

But let us first notice two points wherein Jewish Charity far surpasses Christian. These are *Country* and *Society*. If Jesus preaches love to all men, if Christianity plumes itself more than does any religion, on its humanitarianism, it is at the expense of a love no less sacred, that of country and society. Christianity knows but one country, the world, or rather *Heaven*; and but one society, spiritual society. One's country, its rights, its needs, the limitations it sometimes sets to universal charity, as one right limits another; civil society, truly human, as including bodies and souls united, its special rights, its requirements, the relation between its members, the laws governing these relations, &c.; all these things are ignored by Christianity. Does Christianity recognize the *political enemy?* No. Does it, a social justice? Nor yet this. Now, without a *political* enemy, there can be no country; without social penalties, no society, no justice. A striking example of charity supplanting the rights of justice, is the pardon of the adulteress under the pretext that there was no one who, as being guiltless, could stone her; and it is precisely upon the ruins of both the political and the social necessities that Christianity is based—by snapping the ties that bind man to earth, it takes its flight to spheres where man cannot follow. We shall not, just now, dilate on the menstruum Christianity proves for a social organization. We shall but consider it in its political tendency. While Judaism never omits any of the lower steps that lead to universal charity, but lets the individual, the family, the city, the country, each play its proper part, Christianity leaps over all these, burying them in the abstract gulph it calls the *world, humanity,* or the *Church.*

Let it, then, be no longer asserted that Christianity has taught men greater charity than Judaism. If it has effected this illusion, it is by taking away from the individual, family, and, above all, *country,* those rights which Judaism, with more equity had distributed to each class, to give them all to humanity, thereby losing in *intensity* what it gained in *extent.*

This truth results not alone from many passages and the general spirit of the Gospels, but it takes a special form in the parable of the *Samaritan.* What a name! And why has it not attracted the attention of the savants? They might have asked, why this particular choice; why not select rather a Gentile, a Greek, a Roman— names much better calculated to show off the superiority of the Christian to the Jewish ethics? If we ask this question perhaps we shall obtain a glimpse of the object of the parable, of the ties it wishes to sever for the benefit of the *Church,* of that central stay it would to efface from the bosom of mankind; perhaps we shall find the final word as to this parable, the *abolition of country.* Yes, we ask, why a Samaritan? Is it that Jesus, far from troubling himself yet about his scheme for *all* humanity, far from extending his views beyond Palestine, sought only to establish in the very heart of his country, equality of all races, of all nations, to stifle the country, so to speak, upon its bed of suffering. Did he also share the detestation of his co-patriots, for the tyranny and cruelty of the Gentiles?

We see but one motive in this choice of the Samaritan, viz: to personify in him the **political enemy, and him** only. And truly, if there ever sprung from the bosom of Judaism an implacable political enemy it was the Samaritan. No more fit emblem of this could Jesus have selected. For why does he not choose the idolater, the faithless Israelite, the Roman, at once a religious and political enemy? He wishes to confine himself to the pure political enemy, monotheistic in his creed, no less than the Israelite. Can we doubt the political object Jesus had in view?—the suppression of the spirit of nationality, of the interests and needs of patriotism.

This is not all. Is it the simple idea of duty which Jesus substitutes for this? Does he show us a Samaritan suffering on the highway, neglected, abandoned by a priest, a Levite, and succored by a Pagan or a simple Israelite who knew his duty as to charity better than those of the national hierarchy?

Such an exhibition could mean only that charity and help should be extended to all the unfortunate, be they Samaritans, Jews, or Pagans, and Judaism could have naught to gainsay. But this is not what Jesus presents to us. It is not virtue, duty, absolute charity, that he substitutes for national egotism; it is another egotism, *personal egotism*, the self-love, taken as a rule of conduct in our dealings with others, that he puts in place of the far nobler love of country. For, in this parable, it is a suffering Israelite whom he presents to Israelites, neglected by his own people, and tenderly cared for by a Samaritan. And after having traced a picture, wherein any one of his hearers might at any time play the chief part,—after having touched the most sensitive chords of egotism, of personal preservation; after having shown in the *political enemy* a *personal friend*, and created this perilous variance and artificial perplexity, not based on truth, but which might easily escape the notice of his inexperienced audience—he presses the conclusion: Which of those three is thy neighbor? And the anti-political object of Jesus is so much his concern, that the great danger in which he places his own ethics, escapes his notice. In his impatience to give the Samaritan the title *neighbor*, he takes it away from the Israelite; in his haste to put egotism under obligation to the benefactor, he forgets to curb it towards the enemy; he forgets that love of one's enemy, the cherished theme of another antagonism which he raises between the old law and the new. For if the Samaritan is my neighbor solely on account of his services, the priests and the levites, though they have done me no positive injury, cannot get this title, as they refused me what the Samaritan lavishly bestowed.

CHAPTER VII.

UNIVERSAL CHARITY.

Qualities of the Universal Charity of Judaism.—Not to be found in Christian Charity.—Unity of Man's Origin.—The Worth and Results of this Doctrine in the Teachings of the Pharisees.—Man made after God's Image; Value of the Doctrine.—Unity of Destiny.—Moses and Sophonias.—History of the Primitive Ages.—Humanitarian Character of the Prophecies; can be traced in the Laws.—Justice and Charity equal for all.—Universal Charity of the Pharisees.—Circumstances that Enhance its Value.—Salvation to all Men.—Idea of Man.—Humanitarian Ideas of the Pharisees.—Gentile Greatness equal to that of the High Priest.—Universal Love, Respect for Life, Property, and Reputation—Restrictions.—Political Enemy.—Christ has created the Religious Enemy.

If Christianity has **sacrificed** all for universal charity, has it, at least, succeeded in giving **us the** incomparable ideal for which it is credited ? Has it transcended in this respect the teachings of Judaism, that have, withal, not infringed on the places and rights of country and society ? We dare assert that, in spite of the enormous sacrifices it has made, it gives us an idea of universal charity far less grand than that bequeathed us by Judaism. And we may risk the assertion that the latter, by preserving the rights of country and society, has made charity more active (if possible), more tender, more humane, and in short, more *charitable*. Christianity sees in man but man in the abstract, or even at most but the Christian. But what does the Hebrew not see in him ! Man, his brother, created like himself in the image of God,* the worshiper of the same God, though he be not a disciple of Moses, a father, brother, son; a member, in short, of a family, and above all one that has a country, a nationality;—and as the Jew himself is also a citizen, one of a nation, he can sympathize with the affections appertaining to citizenship and nationality, with the joys and sorrows, virtues and heroisms these relations beget. In a word, Judaism presents a new point of contact for men ; by multiplying relations, it doubles, triples universal charity ; and, instead of the dry abstraction, *man*, that Christianity would have us love, it gives its adherents something more real, more alive and similar to ourselves—something with affections and wants like our own—a father, a citizen, a pat-
riot.

But leaving these restricted considerations of man's character, should Judaism envy Christian ethics ? We need but call to mind one important doctrine, one that is more peculiar to Judaism than to any religion or to any nation, one that is the essential base of universal charity, and without which no philosophy can ever succeed in transfusing man's heart with that tender *brotherly* love, which is its direct consequence—and that is UNITY OF ORIGIN. Let us remember that long before *liberty* and *equality* were spoken of, Israelitic tradition showed how eminently favorable was this great doctrine to these two principles among men. "Why," say in the Talmud, these much-misunderstood Pharisees, "has man got but one origin? It is first, that no one may say to another, 'my father is greater than thine;'* and secondly, that no people or family may, with justification, put another in subjection." Alas! how many such tyrannies have we not in the world! How would it be if each people and race had a separate origin? But mankind from the same parents, how shall that be? And their children all similar in appearance? A grand thought, and one that Genesis, of all books esteemed by men, alone contains.

Man has been created *in the image of God;* he is the king of creation; all ought obey him, that he may ennoble and spiritualize all, by leaving on them traces of the mould from which he himself was struck. Is this representation an exaggeration on our part, or is it truly according to the meaning of the strict Mosaic text? These inimitable doctrines are like the sun, the sky, and other wonders of creation—ever before us, ever familiar to us, and therefore scarce any longer objects of our admiration—otherwise the august ideas that Judaism expresses would forever call forth our unqualified wonder and respect.

There are, however, two important considerations which cannot but enhance the value of these doctrines. The one is the time, the atmosphere wherein they were enunciated; the other, the people to whom they were addressed, and the end sought in diffusing them. Truth herself must indeed have inspired the Hebrew lawgiver, if, in the midst of a people who accounted all close to their frontiers as enemies and barbarians, he was bold enough to proclaim a doctrine that went in the very teeth of that exclusionism in which each nation had entrenched itself. And this people, what was its character? Here it is that the humanitarian side of Israel's existence shines forth. We can easily comprehend that Moses might communicate his great ideas respecting the unity of our origin, the grandeur of man and of his destiny, to some tried disciple, to a school, or, better still, to missionaries who would force them on the attention of an ignorant world. Now had this Jewish people whom he was about to mould, anything of this character? Was it not, in its turn, about to become one of the nations of the

---

* Talmud, Sanhedrim, 38.

East, to have a distinct **existence,** and interests and rights to defend from the constant inroads of its neighbors? Had it not yet to pass through many ages before it could practice the great principles taught it by Moses, or even suspect the fine fruit they could bear? Unquestionably, this universal fraternity, this unity of origin, found on the front of Genesis, have no visible connection with the immediate future of Judaism, and seem to be but dim reminiscences of Paradise existing in the midst of the bloody strifes of national egotisms; or, to speak with more precision, it appears evidently like a coupling-stone to which the non-political side of Mosaism, the religious and moral one, held as to one of its chief stays. But there is another unity which Judaism taught later to men; that is, the *unity of future.* It is the necessary supplement to *unity of origin*, destined to be one day the final terminus of this latter. At the beginning of history, the unity of Moses, the unity of the past; at its end, the unity of Sophonias, the unity of the future. The first is natural unity, the foundation of the other; the second is free moral unity,—a unity of love, faith, thought,—the result at once and the crown of the former. Moses is the prophet of the first, of *man one;* Zephaniah (Sophonias) of *humanity one*, of the collective Adam; and he gives, in the spirit of Moses, the justest formula of this doctrine, saying: *At that time I shall make the lips of people pure lips, that they may all call on the name of the Eternal, and worship him with one* spirit. (Zep. iii. 9.) Is this idea that the Jews were to form of man's origin and of universal fraternity, borne out by the history of the first ages narrated to them by Moses?

It would be unjust to deny that Judaism alone, of all ancient creeds, has given men the history of their origin, of the first ages, and of the various subdivisions of mankind. And besides laying the first stone of that great ethnological structure which has been so expanded in our days, it has revealed, by this very service, its great moral and humanitarian side, and the destiny of this book become universal.

But is not the God whom Moses announces, the God of all men? Are not his justice and care dispensed equally to all? Does he not, in the Mosaic history, interpose continually, avenging fratricide, drowning a corrupt generation, giving Noah laws, directions, which, far from being confined to that people to be formed by Moses, are the inheritance of all mankind.

Is it not "with all his posterity," that God declares to Noah, he established his covenant? (Gen. ix. 9). Is the God of Abraham a fetich, a local, national God, like other gods? Or rather *the God of heaven and earth?* (Gen. xiv. 22). Does not the great patriarch become his prophet and apostle? Does he not importune God on behalf of those wicked people of the plains, with whom his family had no affinity whatever? Does not God himself tell him of his intention respecting these sinners; because, according to the Doctors, it is unworthy of God to punish the *children* without telling their *father*, namely, Abraham, called by the same Pharisees, the father of all nations?* Is not Joseph made to utter language that reveals a Providence ever directing the destiny of nations? "It is God," says he, "who overruled your actions in order to save a great people "†

And why are those Canaanites driven before Israel, from their land? It is here that the God of Moses reveals himself as the *just* God, the God of all men, dealing to the Jew the same justice as to the Canaanite—a doctrine unheard of, incomprehensible, in those early days, and which Judaism alone has made the world understand. Take care, says Moses, that you be not guilty of the same sins and corruptions as are those nations whom you are about to drive out. For, deceive not yourselves, it is neither your virtue nor equity of claim, that gives you the inheritance; it is their iniquity on one side, and on another the oath that God swore to your fathers. Moreover, said he, "if you imitate them the earth will spew you out, as it did them." (Deut. ix. 5; Lev. xviii. 24 and seq.)

Shall we speak of laws? They could not be more charitable, they could not better unite the national existence and particular life of Israel to a love and charity towards all men. Is it nothing that these Gentiles were permitted like the holiest Israelites to offer sacrifices on the altar of the Lord? This is indeed why Moses solicits Pharaoh (Ex. x. 25), this is what the Mosaic laws expressly provide for, requiring the same perfection in the animals from the Pagans as in those from the Israelites; this is what Solomon nobly expresses, when he supplicates God to hear the prayers of the Gentile and stranger (Nochri) who should adore him in the temple he built.‡ Shall we lightly esteem that peaceful sojourn in Palestine assured to the Pagan, on the sole condition of his not worshiping idols, and leaving him at full and complete liberty for aught else; a liberty that extends sometimes to idolatry (as say the Pharisees), as in the case of the female captive who might publicly adore her

---

* Bereshith Rabba, Sect. 49.

† According to Moses and the Prophets, all people are the children of God; only Israel is his first born (Ex. IV. 22). See also, Is. XV. 5; Malachi I. 11; Jerem. X. 7; and all throughout the Psalms.

‡ Kings I., Chap. viii. 41.

gods in Palestine.* And this may be clearly inferred from the text (Lev. xxv. 39) where not only is the sojourn of the stranger anticipated, but his possible want, too, in a strange land, which, with paternal solicitude, Israel is required to relieve; as also to regard him as a proselyte (gher), or merely (according to the Pharisees) as the Pagan (toschab) who dwells in Palestine on the fore-mentioned condition; and he is called by the tender name, *thy brother*, (achikha), better than *neighbor*. But this is not all. "Beware not to take interest in any form, from him; but fear God and act so that *thy brother* can live with thee." We need scarcely say that if this Pagan is a slave, the same legislation applies to him as to the Jew: in the year of Jubilee he infallibly regains his liberty. But, what appears incredible, this same Pagan, this breaker of the Sabbath, this public transgressor, can, with the full sanction of the law, buy an Israelite and hold him as a slave until the Jubilee year. And what is as extraordinary as certain, the law of Moses regulates all these cases, as: An Israelite may be sold to an *idolater* and in Palestine;—nay—even to the *idol* itself, to its *temple* and *worship;* and tradition (the Pharisees) not only has no objection to make, but authorizes this interpretation of the text, in itself very obscure. To the Pharisees is indeed due this interpretation of Leviticus (xxv. 47): *The family of the proselyte is the idolater, the idol itself, to be served, not by adoration or God-worship, but by cutting wood and drawing water for its use.* (Vide Sifra and Raeshi).

We do not mention the remarkable details of these laws, the exhortations given to the Jewish slave of the idolater, not to imitate his master, not to say: "My master worships images; I shall do likewise. My master breaks the Sabbath; so shall I"—to do so would lead us too far from our subject.

The laws protecting the stranger and full of love and charity towards him, are everywhere mentioned: *Love the stranger as yourselves* (Kamokha); for *you* have been strangers in the land of Egypt, for you *know the mind of the stranger*, his sufferings and humiliations;—words as noble as significant, for they make us see in this stranger naught but a man, of a religion, morality, and origin diverse from those of the Israelites, just as were the latter from those of the Egyptians. Not to deceive, not to oppress him, not to withhold unjustly his earnings, being in the same relation to us absolutely as a *brother*. Admirable teaching of the Pharisees, and **of** them only. Not to give him up to his master, not even to an Israelite, if he has escaped from him in a strange land and seeks an asylum with Israel: let him dwell with us and be free; let no Israelite dare to trouble or to cheat him. All this again through the

---

* Talmud, Yebam., fol. 48.

Pharisees. Is not the needy stranger ranked with the poor, the widows and orphans of Israel? Do they not invoke for him, too, the benefit (better than charity) of a right which the law establishes for all,—the tenth part, the corner of the field, and the *dropped ears of corn?*

We have seen the spirit, not only of the Mosaic law, but of the Pharisaical interpretation — these eternally persecuted Pharisees, the objects of implacable hate—and who, notwithstanding, with impassive heart, with serene and immovable spirit, maintain all that is visibly humanitarian in the Mosaic law, and by exhibiting it under a new aspect, and revealing its many-sidedness, bring at last Hebrew charity, human fraternity, into high relief.

Let us now see the Pharisees alone at work, free from all trammels of interpretation, enunciating in the intimacy of instruction, the most independent doctrines, whose publication among the Gentiles, in our modern Europe, they could never have foreseen. Well, these hypocritical Pharisees, of narrow views, ignoble ambition, without heart, enthusiasm, or genius, are not, as we shall see, the Pharisees of history; they are the Pharisees of the Gospel, or rather (what has been best proven) the pseudo Pharisees, taxed, by the true Pharisees, in their oldest books, with hypocrisy. Is it at all wonderful that Jesus should have taught a just, liberal, and generous ethics, and that, by degrees, the world should have entered into the plan of the Gospel? Was Christianity not naturally driven by its failure even with the Jews, to break down the barrier that hitherto separated it from the Gentiles, and to substitute for that refractory Israel—that rebel to the new faith, something, in good sooth, less stubborn? And, above all, had Christianity to contend, like the Pharisees, against the perpetual revolts of the national sentiment from the doctrine of love and charity towards all men? No! To love the Greek, the Roman, or the barbarian, the Christian had not to stifle the bitterest memories of old or recent wrongs; or to shut his eyes to the disgrace or enslavement of his country, he, who found one wherever he went, at Jerusalem no less than at Athens or Rome. Should a good thought, a noble doctrine then, have the same value coming from the Christian as from the Jew? Assuredly not. If historical criticism is just, it must admit that whenever Hebrew charity disengages itself from a thousand obstacles, a thousand adverse sentiments, it rises spontaneously to those hights where all men appear equal. For the doctrine itself is too old, too rooted in the hearts of men to disown it, and men are too loyal, too generous to do so. Is it nothing that these Pharisees in the time of Caligula, Tiberias, and Nero, have seriously debated if the Pagan, keeping his **religion, could** be saved, provided he acknowledged **God and observed** the moral laws? Is it nothing, above all, **that** the affirmative doctrine prevailed in the synagogue (conformable to the belief of all Israel to-day), that Socrates, Plato, and Marcus Aurelius, should have their places in Paradise by the same title as Abraham, Isaac, or Moses? Is it naught that the Pagan, the idolater, should be esteemed as *neighbor*, towards whom fraud is strictly forbidden ; that one law prohibits the robbery of Jew or Pagan ; that they have been so scrupulous as to forbid their inoffensive methods of gaining the good will and esteem of the idolater, to which we already made allusion ; that they extended the Mosaic prohibition of hating the Egyptian, to all the nations who gave Israel an asylum, even while they persecuted him, and this by reason of that fine maxim : "Throw no stone into the well from which thou hast drawn" ; that they have exhorted us to succor the poor, to visit the sick, to bury the Pagan dead—an example followed by the primitive Christians? Who but the Pharisees would have told us — the Mosaic text being silent thereupon — that the seventy bulls sacrificed during the eight days of Tabernacles, were propitiatory offerings for the seventy nations supposed to be on the earth? The Pharisees alone discovered the motive, they who applied to Israel the words of the Psalm : *For my love they persecute me, and I pray for them;* adding : *These are the seventy bulls that were at that time sacrificed, so that the world should not lose one of them ;** and who said : *Oh! if the nations but knew how serviceable to them is the house of God! they would have fortified it all around that it might not be touched.*† And who, moreover, comparing Israel to a dove, give us an idea transcending anything in the Gospels : *Thine eyes resemble the dove's ; as the dove gives its neck to the slayer, so does Israel ; as the dove is made a sin-offering, so Israel atones for the sins of the nations, giving the seventy bulls sacrificed during Tabernacles as an atonement for the Gentiles.*‡ And what a noble sentiment is couched in these words : *Man, created in God's image, how loved is he by him! That love shown him, to be created in that image.*§ And think not their thought extends but to the Israelite ; to him the Talmud immediately after gives a special dignity in the title, *Son*. And is the perfection obtained by the study and practice of the divine law, promised to the Jews only? Not so ! *These are the precepts*, said Moses, *whose practice gives life to man. Does the text*, ask the Pharisees, *say that the priest, the Levite, the Israelite shall live by the law? No! it says* MAN, *that is the Gentile himself.* Without being a convert to Judaism, without even troubling himself about the

---

* Yalkout, page 251. † Midrasth, Rabba, Sect. Emor and Pinchas.
‡ Midrasth Schir haschirim. § Talmud, tr. Aboth. Chap. III.

Mosaic law, provided he studies and practises natural morality, he may equal in dignity the high priest of Judaism. We may boldly say that they never omit an opportunity of illustrating the universality and eminent humanitarianism of their ethics, at the risk even of compromising the election of Israel, his rights or national prejudices.* Could more be required of the highest spirit? Not in vain did David say: "This is the law for man, O Eternal!" (II. Sam. vii. 19). The Pharisees seize the sentence, force from it all its consequences, even those that perhaps its author did not intend. *Law of man*, they say, *and not of priest, Levite, or Jew.* Isaiah (xxvi. 2) says: "Open the doors, and let good men enter, them who uphold their faith." And the Pharisees, commenting on the word *goy*, (nation) say that the reference is not to Jews merely, but to man in general, let the creed or nationality be what it may. "O ye just, praise the Lord," says David (Ps. xxxiii. 1). To this, also, the Pharisees give the same wide interpretation, asserting that the term tzaddikim (the Just) takes in all mankind. And in the 125th Psalm (ver. 5) we read: "O Eternal, heap thy blessings on the just, them who have a good heart!" Another occasion for the Pharisees: *The Just! the Just in general.* But this is not all; the Tanna debe Eliahou advances a step: *I call heaven and earth to witness! Man or woman, freeman or slave, Jew or Pagan, according to their works alone shall the holy spirit come to them.* They point to Aaron as a model, inviting us to have his love towards men and to lead them to the Law. To hate them would be to give up life. Love for humanity knows no restrictions; *we should love idolators even.* And who say so? The Cabalists.

This love should not be sterile. The austere Schammai himself bends to the great Judaic truth and teaches: *Study the Law, and welcome all men with respect.* And according to R. Ismael we should welcome them with *joy*. And how solicitous are they respecting a man's honor! "Let thy neighbor's honor be as dear to thee as is thine own"†—"Despise no one."‡ R. Mathia Ben Harasch and R. Johanan, two ancient doctors, boasted that they had never waited for another's salutation, *were it an idolator's even*. And elsewhere: *Who is truly honorable? He who honors his fellow-creatures.* As to property: *Let the property of thy fellow-man be for thee as sacred as thine own.* "Shouldst thou find thine enemy's ox or ass strayed," said Moses, "thou shalt bring it him;" and that, says R. Yoschia, though

---

* And, indeed, we see in our day the effects of this too-catholic spirit (so to speak), in the facility with which many modern Jews ignore nearly all the restraints and wholesome precepts of their faith as inconsistent with the liberal thought and action that faith ever begets.—[*Trans.*

† Aboth, Chap. 2.   ‡ Aboth, Chap. 4.

he be a pagan or idolator. If the civil law allows usury from the Gentiles, the moral law, through the Pharisees, forbids it: and one of them, a witness, doubtless, if not a victim of pagan cruelties, after seeing at the circus the massacre of his brethren, entered the *Bet hamidrasch* and taught: *Thou shalt not lend on usury even to a stranger.**

Does this, however, mean that Judaism knows no one as enemy and never felt hate? No! and we do not blush to say so. We should not sacrifice the truth, say the Pharisees, even on the altar of the Lord, for the language and memorable examples of the prophets prove but one thing, that God hates, above all, hypocrisy. Yes, the Jew has, or (to speak more accurately) had an enemy, the political one. The Jew, who loved dearly his country, was the natural enemy of all who conspired against it. For such, no truce, no peace, no pardon, as long as there was danger. Against these were the exceptional measures, the martial laws, the terrible decrees, of which we read in the law of Moses or in the books of the Rabbis, attesting one thing only,—*danger*—having but one object,—*the public safety*—recognizing but one right,—the *right of defence*. A right not only lawful, but obligatory above all when it has reference to one's country. Easy for Christianity, that knows no country or nationality to dispute a religious nation's, a sacerdotal kingdom's right of existence and the consequences of that right; to be scandalized whenever the preservation of Israel demands a restriction of that limitless charity which is the final object of the restriction. Israel, with erect head and calm heart, shall never blush for its political character, given it by the God of Christians, nor for the exercise of the rights appertaining thereto. But has Christianity itself no enemies? Here it is, that the deplorable consequences of the absence of a civil polity in that system, unfold themselves. We have seen before that Christianity had to seat itself upon the empty throne, and to transfer there all its religious character and aspirations, and, as it had no political system, to risk the fatal blending of the spiritual with the temporal—of faith with law, of charity with justice, of the *interior* court with the *exterior*, of remorse with policemen, of hell with the scaffold—of which its history, alas! gives us the painful spectacle. Well, we come to one of the worst results of this confusion of things so different. Christianity, that would not have a political enemy, was obliged to have—as soon as it encountered the world—a *religious enemy*.

Yes, the religious enemy is a creation altogether Christian, unknown to Judaism, *impossible* even, the moment it admits that

---

* Talmud, Makkot, f. 24.

eternal salvation is not the exclusive heritage of the Mosaic Law. So this charity, that with the Jew is stopped only by the political enemy, the Christian cannot entertain towards the religious enemy. And let it not be said that this refers to posterior abuses and alterations. The Gospel is there to attest that the genius of Christianity is true to itself from the most remote times. Jesus, who knew so well how to pray for his personal enemies, who would have the Jew love the Samaritan,—that is to say, the Pole to love the Cossack, or the Italian, the Austrian soldier,—Jesus has neither love nor prayer for those not of his church. *I pray not*, he says, *for the world, but for those whom thou hast given me* (John xvii. 9); and elsewhere, *Who is not for me is against me. The tree that bears not fruit shall be cut down and cast into hell-fire.* But where find darker colors, more terrible words, than those he uses to predict the end of the enemies of Christianity? The Church had as yet no soldiers or executioner at its beck, and that is why it has recourse to God, but in what a style! *It is right that God should afflict those who afflict you, and that you should have respite when the Lord Jesus is revealed from heaven . . . in flames of fire, taking vengeance upon those who know not God and obey not the Gospel.* It is because there is no mean between obeying Jesus and being his enemy, that he himself says: *Do you think I am come to establish peace in the world? No, but war. Whosoever will not leave father, mother, brothers, to follow me, is not worthy of me.* Is this execrable end the only one Jesus has in view, as think the detractors of Christianity? Or does he simply mean that war must be the inevitable result of variance of opinion regarding his doctrine? Neither, although there is some truth in the last opinion. He means this only, that *his doctrine being exclusive, his faith intolerant, there being no mean between Christians and the damned, between partisans and enemies, as soon as the former declared for him, they should regard all others as religious enemies, in whom there is nothing to love but* THE SOUL *and its future conversion;* and to attain this end, not to be too particular about the means.

Would we have an example of this difference between Judaism and Christianity in the manner each views its relations to other religions? Paganism accused both at once of being the *enemies of the human race.* How do they receive the accusation? On the one side Tertullien, on the other, the Doctors of the Midrasch comment in styles as singular as diverse. The former, although with proscriptions and constant carnage before him, hesitates not to retort upon his adversaries: *Yes, we are your religious enemies.* The Doctors see in it but the hatred of Paganism towards them;—as to theirs, they see it not, for they feel it not. Only, as this accusation came from Rome, from its Court, its savans, its historians, the

Doctors, who did **not overlook** Rome's intolerant oppression of the world, or the terrible **harvest** of smothered hate and revolt it was everywhere reaping, **took** care, in a remarkable sarcasm, to make Rome, too, a party: *Yes*, say they, *all the world hates Esau; all the world hates Jacob.* And do they think they deserve this hate? They cannot even understand it. They seek in vain *what Israel has done*, to merit the scorn of the Gentiles; they do not even suspect that difference of faith has caused it, so remote from them in the idea of a religious enemy. What tender and pathetic language is this scrap from the Midrasch: *They hated me unjustly, said David. If Esau* (Rome) *hates Jacob, it is because the latter took from him his birthright; but what has he done to the barbarians? To the Philistines? To the Arabs? Did not David say well: They hated me unjustly?* Here is the whole spirit of Judaism. It hates not; so it is astonished that it should be hated, asking with wonder,—not, *What is my creed?* (it never thinks of that)—but only *What have I done?* That is to say, you cannot hate me but for my deeds, and I am innocent. In this cry of Judaism is found all its complaints and tears for centuries. The Pharisees have uttered it from the birth of Christianity, and the persecutors of the Jewish faith still hear repeated in an unerring simplicity: "Tell me what I have done!"

CHAPTER VIII.

PERSONAL ENEMIES.

MOSAIC PRECEPTS AND PHARISAICAL INTERPRETATIONS.—FORGIVENESS OF INJURIES.—MOSES, THE PROPHETS, AND THE PHARISEES.—REWARD OF PARDON.—THE PARDON OF GOD.—DUTIES OF THE INJURER; THOSE OF THE INJURED.—EXAMPLES OF THE PHARISEES.—WHAT ENHANCES THEIR MORALITY.

The restrictions to universal charity can refer to but three classes, viz: to the political, the personal, and the religious enemy. Since it is denied that Judaism has universal charity, and since *special election*, if not Jewish egotism, is spoken of, we have asked ourselves at which of these three classes has Jewish charity perchance stopped. As to the last, we have seen that it is an exotic, unknown to Judaism; while of Christianity, on the contrary, it is the natural product.

Aside from the political enemy, we have seen the stranger, the non-Israelite, our brother, through Adam, ranked with the Israelite himself, and loved in a degree unknown **to** ancient or modern times. There remains, then, only the personal enemy, and to this we direct our attention. Is it true that Judaism does **not** enjoin charity towards our personal enemies, or checks it on account of some miserable interest, some blind antipathy or tyrannical passion? Is it true, in short, that forgiveness of injury, charity, and love towards our enemies are the special traits of Christianity, and constitute a new doctrine introduced by Jesus? This is the apparent inference from his words: (Mat. v. 43), "You have heard that it was said in old times: *Thou shalt love thy neighbor, and hate thine enemy.*" We have, it will be remembered, proved by the best arguments that it is the Law of Moses itself which is here attacked, and that it is the personal enemy alone to which the last words refer; moreover, that no such precept as the last is to be found either in the Law or the Rabbinical writings, but precepts far different in spirit from any such "hate." We have said enough as to the stranger, and now let us see about the personal enemy.

Shall we say that Jesus forgot the most formal prescriptions of the Mosaic law? There are two passages where charity to one's enemy is enjoined, and in both, the Mosaic precept, sufficiently noble in itself, is ten times more exalted and refined through the interpretation of the Pharisees. Singular destiny of their writings—to rebut, at each step, the extraordinary imputations of the Gospel! I say extraordinary, unless they are made against those false Pharisees, rebuked by the Talmud itself, as we have said. "Hate not thy brother inwardly, but censure him for his error, and thou shalt be blameless," says Moses. Would it be less strict in practice? "Take not vengeance, and bear no ill will towards thy fellow-citizens, but love thy neighbor (who is created) like thyself: I am the Everlasting." (Lev. xix. 17, 18). That is, no vengeance on any one, as the last words of the precept show. If the Mosaic language appear sometimes confined to the Jewish circle, it is, I think, because no regular connections existed with those outside it. But hear the Pharisees on this law of *pardon*. "What is vengeance?" ask they: *Lend my thy hook. No, I shall not lend it thee, as thou didst refuse me thine the other day*: here is revenge.—*Lend me thy hook. Yes; though thou didst refuse me thine the other day;* here is ill will." What delicate sentiments, and not found in the Mosaic text! Moses says elsewhere, "Shouldst thou see thine enemy's ox or ass strayed, return it him." . . "Shouldst thou see," say the Pharisees, "thine enemy's ass bending under a burden and withhold thine aid? No; help to relieve his animal." What enemy is here meant? We have already seen; although the Talmud excludes the political enemy, the Mekhilta, a much older, more venerable text, includes not only the political enemy, but the *rene-*

gade idolatrous Jew, the **personal enemy.** But how do the Pharisees understand this precept **as to charity?** *A friend,* they say, *bends under his burden, and* **at the same time** *an enemy asks your help to load.* What strong reasons for preferring to assist the friend! And the **Law** tells us not what we should do; but the Pharisees do, saying expressly that *the enemy must first get our aid.* Are we not right in saying that the Pharisees of history are not those of the Gospel? But Moses does not confine the keeping of his precepts to individuals—he cites, as an example, a whole nation generously pardoning one that had enslaved it for centuries; as in the case of the Egyptians and Jews. And what does Moses enjoin on the latter, just escaped from the yoke of Egypt? Naught but pardon and love to their most cruel foes. Forgetting, with admirable charity, the sanguinary laws that from time to time fell upon his people, Moses sees in their sojourn in Egypt only that an asylum was given to Israel—air, water, and burial ground;—and yet the waters were reddened with their blood, the air still rang with their cries, the earth was bedewed with their tears. The words of Moses: *Thou shalt not hate the Egyptian, for thou hast been a stranger in his land,* would be the bitterest irony, were they not the most refined charity. Is this *to hate one's enemies?* So the prophets did but follow the Mosaic spirit in urging the forgiveness of injury. Did not Solomon say, (Pro. xxiv. 17, 18): "If thou seest thine enemy fall or err, rejoice not, lest the Eternal see it, condemn thee, and bring all the evil on thy head." "The reasonable man is noble, he glories in pardoning injury. (Prov. xix. 11.") And elsewhere (Ib. xvii. 5) "He who rejoiceth at another's misfortune shall himself receive no pardon." "Do not say, 'I shall pay evil with evil;' trust in God and he will assist thee: nor, 'As he has done to me, so shall I to him; I shall pay him according to his deeds (Prov. xx. 22; xxiv. 29).'" Did not his father David say (Ps. vii. 5, 6), "O God, have I paid evil with evil?... Let mine enemy persecute, strike, trample me under foot, and sink my glory for ever!" Was Paul the first to say what we read in the Epistle to the Romans (xii. 20): "If thine enemy hunger, give him to eat, be thirsty, give him to drink, for by so doing thou shalt heap burning coals on his head." No; these are the exact words of Solomon (Prov. xxv. 22) from whom Paul took them. And in Job what language! "I call God to witness that I never rejoiced at mine enemy's hurt (xxxi. 29)." And is not the voice of the Pharisees heard too in this touching concert? Samuel the Little, the colleague of the Gamaliel who was Paul's teacher, adopted as a motto the above-cited words of Solomon, "If thou see thine enemy fall, &c."; repeating them with such a preference that, though Solomon's, they are found in the Mischna under his name. We have seen Ben Azai front the whole law with these words from Genesis, "God created man in his own image," and why he took them as his principle of action in preference to all others. "Give not evil for evil," says the Zohar, "but trust thou in God." If Solomon (Prov. xvii. 13) says, "Evil will always be with the ungrateful man, with him who pays good with evil," the Pharisees push this severity much farther, saying: *Yes, and upon him too who gives evil for evil let the same curse fall. Does not the Law say, If thou see thine enemy's ox strayed, return it to him?*" Moses complains to God, that the Israelites threaten to stone him—"Go," says God, "before all the people"; meaning, as says the Midrasch Rabbi, *Imitate me; does not God pay evil with good? Well, thou too shouldst give Israel good for evil.*

We have seen Moses command his people, whose wounds, from their Egyptian servitude, were still bleeding, to love their enemies, and what is more, their political enemies. Here is an example of the constant reaction of Jewish ethics upon the civil polity, ruling this polity and making it noble and clement. But in whom is the spirit of nationality more quick and keen than in the Pharisees,— as witness the austere dispositions and extreme precautions with which they are reproached? Still, have they never raised themselves to those serene hights, where even the most generous passions are hushed, and where the peace that pervades you leaves nothing possible but love? Yes, the Pharisees have had such moments,—when their weeping country herself could extract from them only a cry of pardon. The Bible says that, on their return from battle, flushed with victory, the Israelite soldiers sang: *Praise the Lord, for his love is everlasting.* A word is, however, wanting to this formula, viz: *for it is good* (KI TOB). Is it chance or design? No one knows. The Pharisees have always regarded it as a sign of mourning, a void in the national joy; for God, they say, rejoices not at the fall of the wicked. A still more delicate thought—On the morning of the day the Egyptians were drowned in the Red Sea, the angels, they say, presented themselves before the throne of God to sing as usual his praise. "Silence," says the Eternal, "my creatures are about to perish in the waters and ye would sing!" The Israelites, too, even to this day, imitate the angels, and on the seventh day of Passover, by the express order of their masters the Pharisees, do not complete the praise-formula (Hallel), their joy is not unalloyed, there is a void—it is sorrow for the Egyptians. Is it at least permitted to invoke divine vengeance upon the head of our persecutors? And did Paul teach something new when he said: *Bless those who persecute you and do not curse them?* The Pharisees say as much, and perhaps more; for not only will they not curse their enemy, but **they will not even complain** of him at the divine bar. "Woe **to the accuser, still more** than to **the** accused!" They add, "If **thou accuse thy** brother, thine own **case** shall be examined before **his; thy** punishment shall precede **that for** which thou askest against **him.**" "What ought we do?" says Paul (Rom. **xii.** 19). "Not **to** take vengeance, *but leave it to God.*" This is a little **different from the** command given in verse 14, *to bless one's enemies;* **still it suffices** for poor human nature, and is moreover what the doctors **require.** "What shall I do to **these** men who persecute me and whom I could hand over to **the** authorities?" asks one of his colleague. "Be resigned," says the other, "and trust in God; he will render them powerless." Or again: "Let the dawn and the evening twilight always find thee in the Beth-Hamidrasch, and they will cease of themselves." Are we allowed **at** least to reply to those who insult us? *Those who answer not insult **by** insult, who bear injury without murmur, **who act from love and** rejoice not at misfortune, for them **has it been written:** 'The friends of God shall be as the sun in all his strength.'*

What is the reward **of** this pardon of our enemies? It is pardon for ourselves. **He** who forgives not, shall not get forgiveness **himself.** We read in Matthew (vi. 14): "If you pardon men their **offenses,** your heavenly Father will pardon yours, but if you," &c. **Is not** this the thousand-times repeated doctrine of the Pharisees? If Moses says that God has tolerance for sin, and pardons rebellion, the Pharisees interpret this after their fashion: "Whose sins does God **pardon? His,** who himself pardons injury." "Whoever is quick, they say, to forgive, his sins too shall be forgiven."

But the **practice of the** Pharisees is no less eloquent. Prayers were offered against a great drought that was producing famine. R. Eliezar, R. Akiba's master, fasts and prays to no purpose; **rain is** far off. R. Akiba fasts likewise and prays: Our Father, our King, we have no other King but thee! Pity us, **O Father,** for thine own **love's** sake! And clouds soon covered the sky and an abundant rain fell. "**Is** it that the one of these doctors is greater or holier than the other?" asks the Talmud. No, it is simply that he forgives more easily. This same Akiba one day asks R. Nehounia the Elder: "By what **merit** hast thou **reached** this great age?" "My son," said the holy old man, "I have never taken presents and never re**fused forgiveness.**" And to a similar question another doctor replied: "**I have never** lain down with hatred to my brother in my breast." "**God** is my witness," said another, "that my head has never rested on **the** pillow, before I pardoned all who injured me;" and through these examples Israel repeats every evening before lying down: "Master **of the world, I pardon** every sin and every wrong done to my person, to my property, to my honor, or to all that I have ; *let no one be punished on my account.*" This is not all, adds another authority: "No person has ever done me evil, that I have not pardoned him, and even from that day done what I could to serve him (Zohar).

The Gospel prescribes also the offender's duty. If thou bring thine offering to the altar, and then remember that thy brother hath aught against thee, be thou first reconciled to thy brother" (Mat. v. 23). Is not this the echo of the ancient Baraita? "Though the offender should sacrifice all the sheep of Arabia, he shall not be free before asking the pardon of the offended." Charity is more than all sacrifices. "I love mercy and not sacrifice," said the prophet. When there is charity, say in their turn the Pharisees, even idolatry is tolerated. The holy name of God is often blotted out by the bitter waters, that the married may be reconciled (Numb. v. 25), say they elsewhere. But in vain shall we search in the Pharisaical writings for what immediately follows the Gospel precept,—viz., the motive of the reconciliation: Agree, says Jesus, quickly with thine adversary, while thou art in the way with him, lest he deliver thee to the judge and the judge deliver thee to the officer, and thou be cast into prison. Verily I say unto thee, Thou shalt by no means come out thence till thou hast paid the last farthing (Mat. v. 25). We would, for the honor of the Jewish name, interpret this passage in a sense altogether spiritual, but the context forbids it, and the parallel passage in Luke is perhaps still more explicit (Luke xii. 58).

Both sides have given our duties on this score. The Gospels, as well as the Talmud, have laid down the methods to be followed in its performance. If thy brother has erred against thee, go and tell him his fault privately ; if he hear thee, thou hast gained thy brother ; but if he will not hear thee, then take with thee one or two more, that in the mouth of two or three witnesses every word may be established ; and if he neglect to hear them, tell it to the Church ; but if he neglect to hear the Church let him be unto thee as a heathen and a publican " (Mat. xviii. 15 and seq.)

Let us now hear the Pharisees. "Sins against our neighbor are not pardoned on the Day of Atonement before our having sought a reconciliation with him. If he refuses forgiveness, return a second and a third time taking with us three witnesses ; if he still remain obstinate, declare to ten persons (the Church) that apologies have been made him and that he refuses to accept them." And furthermore they say : "Let not the injured refuse his forgiveness ; for it has been said of the Gabaonites when they demanded the lives of Saul's children : *They were not of the family of Israel,* whose special character is modesty, mercy, and charity; and for the Pagan only is it written: *They keep their wrath forever* (Amos i. 11). Is it for actual injury only that apologies should be made?—Are they not required as well for ungracious words and proposals? Whoever, says the Talmud, afflicts his neighbor, even by mere words, is obliged to ask his pardon. And if the offended man has died, then take ten persons with thee, stand before his tomb, and say: 'I have sinned against the God of Israel and against thee' (the dead).

Did the Pharisees, so prone to forgiveness, always wait, as was their privilege, till apologies were made them? We have already seen that their custom was to close each day by a general and spontaneous forgiveness. Did they never push their humility to the degree of provoking by all means a reconciliation? Their history furnishes us with more than one example of this noble virtue. It tells us that Rabbi Zera did not cease to put himself in the way of an offender waiting impatiently for the least indication of a wish on his part for reconciliation. But their heroism went further still. Rab (Abba Arikha), the immediate disciple of Juda the Holy, and whose name is one of the most illustrious in Talmudical annals, was affronted by a butcher. Twelve whole months passed and the butcher showed no sign of sorrow. The evening of the day of Atonement at length arrived. What does the Pharisee Doctor do? He simply goes himself to ask pardon of the butcher. He knocks at his door. The butcher, not deigning even to open the door for him, looks out the window "'T is thou, Abba?" he says. "Away with thee, then; I have naught to do with thee." Tradition adds that as he was cutting a cow's head, the knife struck him on the head and he died.

Does all this mean that the Talmud does not show the explosions which suffering, grief, and insult will sometimes cause? We are far from saying so. The Pharisees were not creatures of pure reason, of abstractions made to idealize some virtue; but real living beings, with strong and generous passions and most sensitive to the humiliations and calumnies of which they were constantly the objects. So, nothing wonderful that we have to deplore in the Talmud expressions that ordinary grief could not force from them. And the Gospels—far less excusable however—the Gospels, whose example and worth are a thousand times greater, have they nothing analogous? Does Christian charity never falsify itself? Beside maxims or acts whose merit cannot be too highly appreciated, are truly others that bring these books to a mere human level. In this light must we view the terrible threats Jesus utters against those towns that would not receive his apostles? Must not the tree that **bears no** fruit "be uprooted and cast into hell-fire?" Are not the

Pagans called *dogs*, to whom must not be given the bread intended for the house of Israel? Does not the habitual meekness of Jesus continually falsify itself whenever he has some reproach to make against his enemies the Pharisees? What become of all those tender reproaches, those mild corrections, that patience and indulgence lavished upon thieves and adulterers, when he has to address those detested Pharisees? For them the most cruel imputations, opprobrious epithets of *hypocrites, fools, blind, whited sepulchres, serpents, race of vipers*, and in short the most dreadful imprecations. Father, mother, sisters, wife, children—all must be sacrificed to Jesus to be worthy of him. To follow him, the last duties to the remains of a father must be refused. The brother must deliver the brother to death, the father the child, and children rise against their parents. In judgment-day who shall be placed on the right hand of the son of man; who shall inherit the kingdom prepared from the foundation of the world? Those who shall have done acts of kindness to the *least of his brethren*. And does not the remembrance of unjust persecutions make Paul too sometimes forget the duties and language of charity? One Alexander, a smith, caused him, it appears, some trouble. What does the abolisher of the Law, the greatest of the Apotles, say regarding him? "Alexander, the smith, has caused me much trouble; the Lord shall recompense him according to his deeds" (II Tim. iv. 14). Is this indeed from the same man that wrote, "Bless those who persecute you and curse them not"? (Rom. xii. 14).

And yet how far is the Gospel from the Talmud? The Talmudists yield sometimes to passions far different from those excited by private quarrels with third parties, viz, to the love of country, of nation, enslaved and trodden down by barbarian idolaters. Had Christianity these legitimate excuses of patriotism and nationality? The impatience and imprecations of the former are less personal and consequently less odious. Much more—have the Talmud and the Talmudists as much weight in Judaism, as the apostles in Christianity? The Gospel language is divine and infallible; the Talmudical (in what does not regard precept or dogma) is in no respect so. No Jew concedes inspiration to the Pharisees, as no Christian refuses it to the Gospels. Paul is the Moses of Christians. The Pharisees are the Fathers of the Jewish Church. Can the words of the one have the same weight, the same value, as those of the other? No one will say so. Besides, when the Jewish Church formulized its doctrines it was dominant. All its words and teachings are stamped with the most absolute independence; it had not to conquer souls, its temples overflowed with adherents; it had, above all, no need to refine on some anterior ethics, to flatter the poor and the humble, to **make** a party; it had one already, a very grand **and** imposing one, *the nation*. Whatever it speaks comes simply from **the source** of its doctrine, a natural, spontaneous jet; it has no *poses*, **it** speaks and acts naturally, because, far from thinking it **needs** the assumption of airs of charity and love to excite de**sertions, it** is thwarted from without in its generous impulses; it is **tempted** rather to stifle the words of love ready to escape it, to display an excessive austerity, in order to ward off attacks. We **ask** furthermore, has the ethical charity of the one the same **value as** the charity of the other? Is not one word from the Pharisees worth two from the Gospels? And these words, of which external circumstances give no explanation, and the natural kindness of **the** utterer as little, traversing as they do many generations,—to what are we to ascribe them? To circumstances? Or to men? Either, doubtless, would **have killed** all generous expansion, all charitable impulses. The glory must lawfully revert to but one source, and that is *Judaism*.

CHAPTER IX.

LOVE TO SINNERS.

MEANING OF THE PHARISEES' REPROACH TO JESUS.—PASSAGE FROM EZEKIEL—PHARISEES INTERPRETATION.—BROTHERLY REPROOF; ITS DIFFERENT FORMS.—AARON THE MODEL OF A PRIEST—ABRAHAM THE MODEL OF APOSTLES.—DOCTORS STRIVE TO CONVERT SINNERS.—TESTIMONY OF THE GOSPELS.—PRIVILEGES OF THE CONVERTED.—THE GENTILES.—MEASURE FOR MEASURE.—UNIVERSALITY OF JUDAISM.

Next to charity and the forgiveness of injury, the doctrine most particularly ascribed to Jesus is *love to sinners*. **We** do not examine the political prudence of a new doctrine's preaching the reinstatement of so many proscripts of the ruling Church, and appealing **to** all the religious malcontents, to found, like a new Romulus, a Christian Rome after the method that gave life and glory to Rome Pagan; or (to use a Hebrew example) of imitating Absalom's greetings and promises, in David's anti-chambers, to all the fractious **spirits** he met there. Whatever were the motives, the fact of the proceeding is beyond doubt. Jesus surrounds himself with all sorts of sinners, new patients to whom he brings a cure; he absolves with a word an adulteress, sits to table with the dregs of the people, and equivocates strangely upon the censures of the Pharisees for not drawing near sinners to convert them, but sitting to table and making free with them, before they were cleansed. Against the Pharisees he urges the scriptural and traditional doctrines that they never dreamed of disputing, and that had been ever accredited by the Hebrews. "If a man," he asks his disciples, "have a hundred sheep and one of them go astray, doth he not leave the ninety-nine and go into the mountains to seek the strayed one? and if he find it, he rejoiceth more over it truly than over those that had not strayed" (Mat xviii, 12). In Luke we have this parable too, with others of the same kind: that of the woman who lost a piece of silver, and that of the prodigal son. Well! we have, in a passage from the prophets, both the idea and simile that Jesus employs against the descendants and imitators of the prophets: "The word of the Lord came unto me," says Ezekiel; "Son of man prophesy against the shepherds of Israel and say to them: woe to the shepherds of Israel who feed only themselves! Should not the shepherds feed the flocks? Ye eat the fat, and ye clothe yourselves with the wool; ye kill the fat sheep, and ye feed not the flock. Ye have not healed that which was sick, neither have ye bound up the limb of the wounded. Ye have not brought again the strayed *nor sought for the lost*, but with force and cruelty have ye ruled them. And they were scattered because without a shepherd, and because a prey to all the beasts of the fields. My sheep wandered through all the mountains and high hills, and were scattered over the face of the earth. . . . Thus said the Lord God: I shall demand my sheep and seek them: as the shepherd, when with his sheep, seeketh the strayed ones, so shall I seek my sheep and draw them from the places to which they have strayed in the cloudy and dark day. . . . I shall seek the lost and bring again those that were hidden, and bind the broken limbs of the wounded. . . . As for you, my flock, behold! I am about to separate the sheep, the rams and the he-goats." (From this comes the saying of Jesus as to the separation of the sheep from the goats at the last judgment.) Here is unquestionably the model which long preceded Jesus and his doctrine, and which he could not forget in his utterances. But we must examine more closely what the Pharisees taught on this subject and see if they entertained the aversion and estrangemnent towards the sinner with which the Gospels reproach them.

Two things appear from Jesus' utterances on this subject: First, the duty of working for the conversion of sinners and the charity we should entertain towards them; and second, the greatness of those same sinners when converted, the place they occupy in God's love, and the glorious crown promised them. We shall not inquire of the Bible if these ideas are unknown to the Pharisees, as we have just seen what Ezekiel writes. There is, however, a precept that forms a transition from the Bible thoughts on this question to the Pharisaical ones, viz., fraternal correction; and it is one of those subjects which, without tradition, lose some of their value in the Mosaic Law. Its literal signification is an amicable adjustment of disputes between friends. It is Pharisaical tradition alone that points out the duty of striving for the conversion of sinners, rigorously enjoining its practice, even at the sacrifice of our self-love, at the risk of the rudest affronts,—in short, at every hazard save that of humiliating the sinner. For, beside the precept to fraternal admonition, the Pharisees see a provision and limitation against abuse, in the words of Moses as interpreted by them: "Reprove him, but always so that thou dost not expose thyself to sin; that is, to humiliate and put to shame thy neighbor." And, what is remarkable, it is this very subject that draws from the Pharisees the assertion upon which Jesus bases his excessive tolerance towards the sinner, viz: that no one is free from sin, and that consequently no one has the right to judge too severely his neighbor.

Did not Rabbi Tryphon say, respecting this precept: "I should be much surprised, were there any in this generation who know how to reprove. I should be much more so, replies another, were there any who know how to profit by a reproof; for my part, I should be so only were I told that some have the right to reprove; for, if one say to another: 'Take out the straw that is in thine eye,' he would get for answer: 'Take out the beam that is in thine own.'"* If I mistake not, here are both the language and the ideas of the Gospel, less the abuse there made of them.

We shall not mention the Hebrew institutions whose only object was to bring the strayed to the right way; or that exhortation to which Jesus owed many an inspiration and which rang continually through the portico of the temple, in the synagogues and public places, when, in time of great public calamity, the whole people were assembled about the oldest and most venerable Doctors, who spoke to the weeping multitude the following words preserved in the Mischna: † "My brothers, it is neither hair-cloth nor fasting that obtains pardon for you; for the Bible says not that God had regard to the hair-cloth and fasting of the Ninevites, but truly to their repentance and amendment. And it is moreover written (Joel ii, 13), *Rend your hearts and not your garments.*" The Pharisees had so high an idea of the conversion of sinners, that the words of the prophet respecting Aaron, viz., "he drew many from sin," ‡ suffice

---

* Talmud Arachin, folio 16.   † Talmud Taanith, folio 15, &c.   ‡ Malachi, ii. 6.

them to build a splendid edifice, that need not envy the most tender Gospel effusions in favor of sinners. "How," they ask, "did Aaron win men from sin? Whenever he found that any one was following wrong paths, he sought carefully such a one's friendship and society. What was the result? The sinner said to himself: Oh! if the holy priest knew my conduct, how he would flee me! And it was this constant thought that brought him gradually to repentance."*

And is Aaron the only friend of sinners mentioned by the Pharisees? David had already said, "I shall teach thy ways to the wicked that they may return to thee (Ps. ii. 15). This species of spiritualization which tradition mentions respecting Bible personages is of much older date; it reaches even to Abraham. It is perhaps difficult to find in Genesis anything resembling an *apostleship* of the great patriarch. Some phrase, indeed, occasionally invests the pastor, the Arab Melkh, the soldier, the patriarch, with a far more splendid halo than the gold and silver one given him by the Bible. But ten to one that even a sharp criticism lie hard set to discover in tradition a clear trace of the apostleship of Abraham. If such is believed to-day and is admitted even by the Church, it is derived from the Pharisees; to these belong the honor; their genius it is, that has changed "the slaves got at Haran" into *souls of sinners gained at Haran*,† Could such transformations be possible for those who did not esteem the conversion of sinners as one of the highest and holiest virtues? And accordingly how profuse and eloquent are their exhortations. "Whoever shall save his neighbor for the glory of God, shall merit the heritage of the Lord."‡

To love men and to bring them close to the law were precepts upon which Hillel and Schammai were always agreed §. The Zohar, above all, utters words surpassingly sublime and tender: "It is the duty of the righteous man to pursue the wicked one and reconquer him at any cost; this is the highest homage he can pay the Eternal. . . Oh! did the world but know what merit it could acquire by the conversion of the impious, it would cling to their steps as to *life*." As to a certain Rabbi Meir (who gave way sometimes to passion, like Paul against the smith Alexander), a crowd of Doctors see in the sinner only a sick brother whom they *must* cure. We shall cite here but three examples of this. The first is of the woman Berouria, who, in spite of the grammatical rendering, found in the Psalms, that we ought to pray for the death of *sin* and not for that of the *sinner* ‖. The other is much more ancient, being the

* Yalkout, ii. 87 (Venice Edition).   † Gen. xii. 5—Talmud Sanhed. fol. 99, &c.
‡ Talmud Tamid, fol. 28.   § Aboth, Chap. ii.   ‖ Berachoth, fol 10.

wife of Abba Hilkiya, who prayed incessantly for the conversion of some sinful acquaintance.* The Doctor is Rabbi Zera, who sought the company of sinners to reform them, and was so familiar with them that he incurred the censure of his colleagues. But the Rabbi died and then these wretched people said in their hearts : Hitherto the little Doctor with burnt feet prayed for us, but now who is going to pray for us? God touched their hearts and they repented. † But what better testimony can we have than that of the Gospels? Well, the Gospels themselves attest most solemnly the extreme zeal of the Pharisees for the conversion of the Gentiles. "Woe to you (cries Jesus,) Scribes and Pharisees, hypocrites! for you scour sea and land to make one proselyte, and when you get him you make him twofold more the child of hell than yourselves!"

Once converted, the sinner need not envy the lot of the most just! Jesus, as we have seen, is eager to place him above the innocent, and that always, without observing the limits which common sense, justice and morality impose, and which the Pharisees are careful not to overstep. Can, indeed, every sort of convert aspire to the same degree of happiness and reward that attends the most just? Jesus, who wishes to attract to him, at any price, sinners, has no reserve. Not so, the wiser Pharisees. This is why the converted sinner, about whom we are going to speak, is the converted sinner eminently ; he who has filled all the conditions of a great penitence,—who, in a year or an hour of heroism and self-denial effaces a whole life of licentiousness or crime. Such a convert, indeed, has no more eloquent eulogists or better friends than the Pharisees. *One hour of penitence and good works in this world, say they, is more worth than a whole life in the world to come;* ‡ doubtless, because it can win the latter. Is it that the Pharisees would not have conceded merit to works and exterior acts, as one might suppose from the imputations of the Gospel? Far from it! The Pharisees are so far from being satisfied with a mere formulism, with acts originating in no conviction or feeling, that they have established an important distinction with respect to the indispensable interior changes—one that might surprise us, did we not already know that the epithet, "Religion of love," belongs not exclusively to Christianity. This distinction is : if it be through fear of the power, the wrath, or even the greatness of God that a sinner repents, the sins he has committed will be reckoned against him only as *faults*, as mere omissions ; but if it be through a disinterested love of God and of his perfections, then his sins are counted as *merits ;* whatever up to that time was a cause of condemnation, now becomes a title to glory and eternal happiness §. And what is this happiness?

* Taanith, fol. 23.　† Sanhed, fol. 37.　‡ Aboth, Chap. iv.　§ Talmud, Yoma, fol. 86.

According to the most moderate of the Doctors, it is all the promises made by the prophets to Israel *. "All the prophecies," say they, "refer but to penitents; as to the just themselves, for them it is written: 'No eye,' O God, 'but thine, has seen their reward.'" But other Doctors go much further, and hesitate not to tell us, "the just, the perfect, will not be worthy to sit with penitents in the world to come." †

To cite all we could on this subject would be never to end. They who said, "we must take, as leader, one who has frightful reptiles on his back" (a sinful past), so that if he grew proud, they could say to him, *look behind!*—have not blushed to give us as guides and models men come from the worst slime of immorality and Paganism. For them, what else is the father of the human race but a penitent. Abraham, his father Tarech, his son Ishmael, Reuben, one of the twelve fathers of the nation, Aaron himself, who so well taught others to repent, have they not been sinners? Is not David, the King of Israel, the Pharisees' representative of all sinners? ‡ Who are sunk deeper in all kinds of sin than Achab and Manassah? Still they are models of penitence, whom the Pharisees praise to envy §. And who are Schemaia and Abtalion, the fathers and oracles of the Pharisaical school, if not converted Pagans? And did pure Israelitic blood flow in the veins of Bag-Bag and Ben Hehe—him who said: "The reward shall be proportioned to the suffering," ‖—and of the great Chaldean commentator Ankylos, and Rabbis Akiba and Meir, and many more? The Pharisees honor themselves by saying that one came from the Amalekite, Aman; another from Sennacherib; another yet, from Sisera, who were not, as we know, heroes of sanctity. Rabbi Simeon Ben Lakish was a highway robber, and Rabbi Eleazar Ben Dourdeya a libertine. And how pathetic the language of Juda, the Holy, as to the latter. On being told that this sinner, after a penitence of a few moments, had died, he wept and said: "There are those who gain eternal happiness, only after long years of toil; but, on the other hand, there are some who gain it in a few moments." ¶

And is the lot of converted Pagans inferior? This God of Israel, this local and national fetich that Voltaire and others have imagined, does not disdain to send his prophet to convert the Ninevites. "Thou truly, hast had pity for this gourd that cost thee neither labor nor trouble," said he to this Jew who could not rise to the

---

* Talmud Sanhed. fol. 99.   † Talmud Berach, fol. 34.   ‡ Talmud Aboda Zara, fol. 5.
§ ke Rabbi Eliezer, xli.   ‖ Aboth, Chap. v.   ¶ Talmud Aboda Zara, 17.

divine thoughts, "And should **not** I spare that great city Nineveh wherein are more **than six** score thousand souls?" *

What example **did** the Pharisees, in their public discussions, set before the elect people? We have seen;—that of Nineveh.

Why is Israel called the people of the God of Abraham, rather than of the God of Isaac or Jacob? Because Abraham was the *first proselyte* †, and that wherever there are true believers *there* are God's people—a noble idea, which Christianity has turned against the Pharisaical Judaism that instructed it. Why are proselytes called the *loved* of God, while the just Israelites are called only *they who love God?* "Because," replies R. Simeon Ben Jochai (the chief of the cabalistic school from which we believe Jesus learned everything), "proselytes surpass Israelites as much as those loved of God surpass those who simply love him"‡. "Oh!" he adds, "how God loves proselytes; on whom are lavished all the names with which Israel has been honored, viz: *servant, minister, friend!*

Abraham, David, were proud to be called proselytes. Has not the latter said (Ps. cxlvi. 9): "God is the guardian of proselytes?" But how expressive the parable used by R. Simeon Ben Jochai to express the divine predeliction for reformed Gentiles! The Gospel has nothing like it. "A father of a family had a flock that went every day to feed, and returned at night. Once a wild goat joined the flock and would not go away from it. The sheep were led to the park, with the goat following; in the morning they were taken to the fields, and the goat still kept with them. So that the father conceived for the goat a great love; he never absented himself from his folks without telling them to allow the goat to feed at his pleasure, and not to strike or ill-treat him. And when the goat returned in the evening, the master himself gave him drink. One day the servants said: "Master, thou hast bucks, tame goats and lambs in abundance, why this love for the wild goat?" The master replied: "The former follow but their nature, which decrees them to feed, during the day, on the fields, and to return, in the evening, to the park. But the abode of wild goats is the forest. How should I not love him, that has given up his forest, his vast plains, his liberty and his comrades to shut himself up in my park?"§ We need not make the application. The history of the Pharisees, like that of Christianity, gives us numerous instances of the sudden conversion of the Gentiles charged with the execution of some bloody decree against the person of the Rabbis. Thus the jailer of Rabbi Chanina Ben Teradion threw himself into the fire with his victim ‖, and

---

* Jonas, fin.   † Talmud Succoth, 49,   ‡ Mechilta—Yalcot, vol. I, fol. 94.
§ Bamidbar Rabba, Sect. viii.   ‖ Talmud Abode Zara, f. 18.

the officer charged with the execution of the death-sentence, upon Rabban Gamaliel, threw himself from the top of the roof and was killed—converts both, who had already secretly professed Judaism, saving themselves by death from a terrible alternative.

The last case was that of Kattia bar Schalom. His opposition to a tyrannical decree against the Jews caused him to be suspected of Jewish magic and to be condemned to the wild beasts. He was led to punishment, when a matron, entertaining also, as it seems, Jewish sentiments, and recognizing him by some Jewish sign perhaps, cried out: "Poor vessel, that goes away without paying tollage!" Kattia understanding the words, drew a knife from his pocket, cut the prepuce and cried, "Now that I have paid my toll I may pass." At his death a supernatural voice was heard saying: "Kattia Bar Schalom has attained life eternal."

A maxim in Matthew (viii. 1) has some affinity to the love for sinners: "Judge not, that you may not be judged." It must be an old Jewish one, since Joshua Ben Perachia (whom the Talmud asserts was Jesus' Teacher), and Hillel repeated it. The former taught: "Judge all men favorably." The other, "Judge not thy neighbor as long as thou art not in his place (in the same situation). "For," adds Jesus, "as thou metest, so shall it be meted unto thee, and as thou judgest so shalt thou be judged." As to the last idea, it forms, with the Pharisees, the conclusion of all favorable decisions: "As thou hast judged leniently thy neighbor, be thou too mercifully judged in heaven." And is it not also contained in that other maxim already cited: "Whoever invokes the judgment of God upon his neighbor, shall have his own case first examined."

But Jesus has also said: "As thou givest, so shall it be given unto thee." The language and idea are purely Pharisaical—a thought most familiar to this school: "As man measures so shall it be measured unto him," says the Talmud;* "and not only the entire measure but any part as well. . . . If all rules fail, one will stand, and that is *measure for measure*." Is it not the last rule of God's justice? So, the Pharisees see it everywhere in history. If the cotemporaries of Noah were drowned, it was because they arrogated the power of bringing rain.† If Miriam deserved that all Israel stopped traveling for seven days, it was because she stopped some moments to watch the cradle of Moses exposed on the Nile.‡ If Samson had his eyes put out, it was because he consulted but them in the choice of a wife. If Absalom was hung by his hair, it was because he was vain of its beauty. If the woman suspected

---

* Talmud Sota, I, fol. 8.   † Talmud Sanhedrim, fol. 108.   ‡ Talmud Sota, fol. 11.

of adultery make an offering of barley without oil or incense, it is because she has descended to the level of the beasts that eat barley. If the incredulous captain was crushed to death by the crowd of buyers, it was because he mocked Elisha's promise of plenty, saying: "Shall God open windows in the sky."* And was not Hillel himself inspired with the same thought, when addressing a crane that he saw floating on the waters, he said : " Because thou hast drowned, hast thou in turn been drowned, and such shall be likewise the fate of thy murderers."†

What we have said is a full answer to the old charge against the Pharisees, that they would monopolize virtue and eternal happiness because Israel is a people elect and Abraham its father. That such a charge was the favorite theme of the early Christians cannot be denied; this was most frequently employed as a reason to reject Judaism and to pave the way for their apostleship to the Gentiles. From the time of Jesus echoed in Palestine, " Do not say to yourselves, ' We have Abraham for our father;' for I say to you God can raise from these stones even, children to Abraham." (Mat. iii. 9.) Paul calls Abraham, "father of the circumcision; that is to say, of those not only circumcised, but who likewise adhere to the faith of our father." (Rom. iv. 12.) And more clearly in chapter 9, verse 6: " But all the descendants of Israel are not for that reason of Israel; nor are they all *children* because they are the *seed* of Abraham. But in Isaac is it that his posterity should be reckoned; that is to say, the children only of the promise are represented in his seed." And again (Rom. ii, 11), " For God has no respect to persons;" and further on (iv. 11), " Abraham received the sign of circumcision as a seal of his righteousness by faith while uncircumcised, that he might be the father of all those who believe though they be uncircumcised." And in the 17th verse, " As it is written, I have made thee a father of many nations." This slur as to Jewish election even free criticism has sometimes made, without reflecting that if the Jews have election it is that they may be less exclusive— that they may become *universal*. Yes, if they were never fused with mankind at any time or place it is that they might be better united in heart and spirit to mankind in all times and places; and had this fusion taken place, that would have been the end of their priestly mission and of the religious future of mankind. But does not the aspiration to this universality break forth and show itself in the history and teachings of the Jews ? We have spoken sufficiently of it, **when** treating of *Man* and the *Gentiles*. We shall now but add a few **special** maxims to what we have already said

---

* **II Kings,** vii—Sanghed, folio 90. † Aboth ii.

We have seen that, with the Pharisees, whoever **are** modest, merciful, charitable, are of the race of Abraham, and that whoever are otherwise, be they Israelites or not, have no share with the former. If there be any term which, on every occasion, the Pharisees set over that of Israel, it is *man*. David had said : " God is good to Israel, to men with pure hearts." The Zohar and the Midrasch eagerly draw this conclusion from the statement, " *God is good to Israel ;* is it to all those bearing the name ? By no means, but to those alone who are sinless, *to men with pure hearts.*" " God loves the just," it is said elsewhere. " Why ?" ask the Pharisees. " Because they are not so by heritage, because virtue is not hereditary." The sacerdotal office is a family gift. Can any one be priest or Levite ? No ; but he who wishes to be just, though a Pagan, can be so. Why ? because virtue is not an inheritance. This is why *God loves the just.* " Why," ask our doctors, " has the Law been compared to the *tree of life?* Because, as the tree of life stretches it branches over all who enter Paradise, so the law covers with its shade all who come into the world."*

It is remarkable that Paul adopts the Pharisaical method of interpretation and grammatical distinctions, to exaggerate even the value set on virtue by the Pharisees, and to tear the old diploma of Jewish election. What does he mean when he asserts that, for being the *seed* of Abraham all are not on that account his *children?* This is the well known distinction which the Pharisees had made between the legal value of the word Zera, *seed,* and BEN, *child;* understanding by the first, all natural descendants, legitimate or otherwise, just or not ; and by child, the special title of those worthy the name in either a legal or civil point of view. What does he mean when he adds that through Isaac should be reckoned the posterity of Abraham ? Nothing but what the Pharisees had already observed, namely, a somewhat obsolete form of expression, which originated with the Doctors the interpretation : " *In Isaac,* yet not *all Isaac,*" excluding consequently Esau. Singular destiny of the Pharisaical language and ideas, to furnish the Gospels all their weapons to smite spiritually old Israel, as did the Romans corporally in its external life! Singular fate of the Jerusalem of the Pharisees, harrassed at once by Pagan Rome in the zenith of its power, and by Christian Rome in its cradle, practicing thenceforth its parricidal child's play—the one, spoiling it of its royal robe, the other, of the tiara of its eternal priesthood ! This Pharisaical Jerusalem, denounced *as the enemy of the human race,* esteemed itself but as the last called of the nations, as their vicar, their religious

---

* Midrasch, Techillim, explanatory of Ps. I. 3.

representative, **so far was it from** aspiring to an exclusive election inimical to humanity. **So it has** not ceased to express its thought under every form. **If God** appears to Israel on Sanai and gives him the Law, **it is** because *Edom, Ishmael, all the other nations* of the world had **been** called before him, and because the law is destined to **become** the *universal law* when the will of God is accomplished. **The** Pharisees have a parable of which we have an inverted copy in the Gospels on the subject of the rejection of Israel. The Gospel **one** is known; it is that of a king who calls to a solemn feast his ministers, nobles, and distinguished men, but in vain; no one comes. Then he orders his servants: go into the highways and call everybody without distinction. Is not the sense evident? But let us hear the Pharisees: "A king gave a great dinner and invited all his guests. No one came at the appointed hour. They were waited for a long time, but in vain. At length, towards evening, some guests appeared; the king received them with joy, and thanked them for coming, saying, 'Were it not for you this fine feast would be lost; I should have to throw it away.' Thus, they say, has God spoken to Israel: 'Thanks; for without thee to whom should I have **given** the great treasure I have prepared for the future?'"*

We need not comment on the parables; all can see the resemblance and the vast difference caused by the adverse position Christianity assumed. In view of these parables we ask which of the two —the first assuming the original intention of God to be *the exclusion of the human race* and their *admission* to be but the accident of Israel's refusal,—the second, making God's first thought to be one of justice, love, and universal charity—one that sees in the election of Israel only a temporary expedient, an imperfect realization of the divine idea—which, we ask, is the more noble, humanitarian, and worthy of Deity? The answer, we think, is easy.

* Midrash Tehillim.

CHAPTER X.

TRUST IN GOD.
[CONCLUSION.]

TRUST PREACHED BY JESUS—ITS EXTRAVAGANCE.—TWO PHARISAICAL SCHOOLS—THE JEWISH PROTOTYPES OF THE GOSPEL TRUST.—THE DOGMATIC FICTION, MAKING MAN FREE FROM TOIL.—TOIL IN JUDAISM AND IN CHRISTIANITY.—PHARISAICAL EXAMPLES.—THE OBJECT OF LIFE; *the glory of God.*—OUR METHOD OF COMPARING THE TWO SYSTEMS OF MORALITY.—JUDGMENT OF MR. SALVADOR.—ITS INACCURACY.—HIS MODE OF CHARACTERIZING THE SYSTEMS.—MAN AND WOMAN.—The HOUSE AND THE CLOISTER.

After charity and love towards our enemies we come naturally to speak of trust in God. Here, as elsewhere, has Christianity taken the most ascetic doctrines of the Jews, those which governed a special sect, a society of meditatists, to make them general rules for human life; here, as elsewhere, has Christianity transferred the doctrines and ethics of the Essenes to the midst of society, of its concerns and needs; here, in short, as elsewhere, it has pushed ideas to an extreme. As long as it was contented with the maxim: "Enough for each day is the evil thereof," it but echoed the teachings of the old Ben Sirach: "Be not troubled about the ills of to-morrow, for thou knowest not what may happen to-day;"* and of the Pharisees who had said: "To each period its evil;" but it is quite another thing to say: "Take no regard for your life, for what you shall eat or drink" (Mat. vi. 25 and seq.; Luke xii. 22 and seq). Consider the birds of the air, they neither sow, nor reap, nor store away, and yet your Heavenly Father feeds them; are you not much more worth than they? And who among you, by taking thought, can add to his stature one cubit? And why are ye concerned for raiment? See the lilies how they grow; they toil not, they spin not, and yet I say unto you Solomon in all his glory was not arrayed like one of these. If, then, God so clothe the grass which is to-day in the field and to-morrow is cast into the oven, shall he not much more clothe you, ye of little faith? Seek not what ye shall eat or wherewith ye shall be clothed?"

When Jesus uttered these words, he left not Judaism, he spoke no unknown doctrine; on the contrary, he took decided part with one of the two schools that then divided Pharisaism. A marked distinction separated the school of Rabbi Ismael from that of Rabbi Simeon Ben Jochai. While the former, attached to the general spirit of Judaism, would associate the toil of the Law and of contemplation with that of civilization and art, the latter—taking as its

---

* Talmud Sanhed. fol. 106.

chief R. Simeon, **the prince of ascetics, the avowed author of that** Cabala which **has given Christianity** everything—spoke a very **different** language. It said, after its master : **If** man tills the ground, harvests, **and** occupies himself with all material works as they present themselves in their seasons, how shall he find time to study the **Law?** No; when Israelites do the will of their heavenly Father, **their work** is done for them by the hands of others ; but when they **are** recreant to that will, they must perform not only their own but **the** work of others as well."* R. Simeon spoke as an ascetic, from **the** special code perhaps of his sect, which was truly that of the Essenes or Cabalists. However that may be, the genius of Judaism has always inclined decidedly to the side of R. Ismael

Abbaye, one of the greatest Talmudists, gives admirably the definitive judgment of Judaism on this dispute between the two equally venerable masters. "Many," says he, "have done as Rabbi Ismael directs, and attained their object; many others have followed the doctrine of **R. Simeon** and have not attained theirs."†

But this doctrine, so exaggerated by Jesus, has a date anterior to that of the contest between the Rabbis. It may be found in those fine counsels given by R. Meir, remarkably qualified though, by a recommendation to an occupation : " Let a man always teach his son **an** honorable and easy trade; above all, pray to Him to whom all wealth belongs ; for in every trade are found, now poverty, now abundance ; neither depends on industry itself, but on a man's deserts." And here the parable used by Jesus appears without danger, tempered as it is by the preceding advice. " Were the beasts or birds," adds the Talmud, " ever seen plying trades ? Yet they **get** their food without difficulty, though created but for my use. How much more reasonable that I too should find my food without difficulty, created as I have been to serve the Eternal¡! If I find it not, it is because I have done evil, because I myself have sullied the foundation of blessings."‡ Do we wish something bearing a closer likeness to the doctrine of Jesus? **Hear the ancient** Doctor Nehorai, of whom the Mischna makes mention **in the ethics** of the Fathers, and who, from all we know, belonged, very probably, to the sect of the Essenes **: " I** shall give up," he says, " all arts and trades to teach my son the Law, for we are nourished on its products, (by its merits) in this world, and the principal is kept for us in the next." Jesus adds, " Do not ask, what shall we eat or drink ?" calling those who do so, *people of little faith*. Who cannot recognize here the old Pharisaical maxim, " Whoever having bread in his basket, says,

---

* Talmud Berachoth, fol. 35. † **Talmud, Berachot.** ‡ Ibid, Kiddoushin, fol. 82.

What shall I eat or drink to-morrow? is a man of little faith."* But who does not see the difference, also; the man of little faith, according to Judaism, is he who, having bread in his basket, yet doubts as to his subsistence for the morrow; the Christian example is simply he who foresees, or the *true sage*.† Above all, beside the extravagant trust in God pushed to improvidence, beside the instance given us of the *beasts in the fields*, not a word in the Gospels to temper declarations so absolute, to encourage us to labor or to condemn idleness. It is not too much to say that we shall search in vain the Gospels, for any resemblance to the great principles incessantly preached by Judaism. Can we wonder that a doctrine, founded on the supposition of a physical state totally different from ours, on the expectation of a general transformation close at hand, that should restore the world to its pre-Adamite condition, wherein "toil in the sweat of the brow" (the consequence of sin) would be unnecessary—should speak as though we were already in the full enjoyment of Paradise, or indeed of the resurrection-era seen, in the far distance by the Pharisees also, and finely pictured in their legends, when bread and the tissues of Mylet should come ready-made from the bosom of the earth,‡ and the Flora and Fauna of our planet be totally changed?

The consecration of labor would be as strange for Christianity as would be its absence in Judaism; which, far from teaching the incarnation of the Word in an *individual*, sees its embodiment in *doctrine*; which, far from making our salvation depend upon the imputation to us of the merits of another, makes each one his own true redeemer; and which, instead of limiting redemption to a point of history, to the hours of Jesus' crucifixion, realizes and develops it always and everywhere through a succession of ages. Consequently, how great the homage paid to labor! What an air of ease, activity, and wealth in the bosom of Judaism! In it, we seem to be in the house of a patriarch; here are agriculture, arts, commerce, gold, silver, cattle; through all is religion, blessing and exalting all things by showing their final end in eternity. Christianity is eternity itself, a forced exotic in the climate of Time, with its immobility, repose, and ceaseless *Sabbath*. In it, we breathe the air of a cloister; here is religion, faith, supplanting all things; the end confounded with the means; labor preceded by repose. Need we say that it is the very antithesis of Judaism? We do not speak of the Bible. Labor, arts, wealth, the goods of life, are so valued there, to the exclusion of all else that Biblical Judaism has been charged with pure materialism by those who mistook the Pentateuch for the

---

* Talmud, Sota, 48. † Ibid, Tamid, 32. ‡ Ibid, Shabbath, 30, &c.

religious instead of **the civil code of the Jews.** The past, the present, the future of Judaism, all its history, its fears and hopes, breathe of labor, abundance, and the good things of life. Upon this we need not expatiate, for other pens have well elucidated it. But what merits well the attention of the philosophical reader is that in spite of the powerful action of causes tending to make the Pharisees forget the Biblical teachings, in spite of the ever-increasing sway of pure speculation, in spite of the enthronement of a spiritual theology in the centre of Judaism, in spite of a belief in immortality, in a future life, in a resurrection, in all the doctrines upon which Christianity has made shipwreck, in spite of political misfortunes and the continual overthrow of its temporal hopes,—Judaism has resisted all the enervating influences, all the temptations to an excessive mysticism, all the delusions that each day was bringing forth. In vain did the world rage against the old weak Israel; Israel, that in its infancy struggled with the angel, found always new force to oppose to the world. In vain did this world display before it all that was horrible and revolting—destitution, torture, slavery—nothing could shake its faith in the *world*, never by it made the synonym of *evil* and *sin*. The more Judaic life was compressed, the more vigorously it rebounded from its falls, reacting with new energy against the causes that should seemingly have exasperated it against the world. The world! Christianity showers upon this its curses, as soon as its lips touch the cup of misery—which Judaism drains to the dregs, its faith in the world unshaken. The blessing to the first man ever rings in the ears of the latter: "Till the earth, subdue it, rule over the fishes, the birds, and all the animals on the earth." And Israel replies by *obedience*, that is by LABOR!" We need not say what the Bible contains as to the necessity, the duty, the utility of labor. The book is within the reach of all. What is wonderful is that the unanimous sentiment of the Pharisees has not deviated a point from the Bible doctrine. From the time of Schemaia, the master of the two chiefs of Pharisaism, the Synagogue has no better counsel to give than to *love work* and to *flee grandeur*.* If Moses exhorts us to choose *life*, the Pharisees see in this *industry*.† If Solomon invites us "to live joyfully with the wife whom thou lovest," the Pharisees see in this wife *the Law*, and in this living *industry*, which two should not be separated.‡ Does not the teaching of his children some art or trade constitute, with circumcision and the study of the Law, one of a father's first duties towards them? Is it not, according to the Pharisees, to make one's child a **robber**, not to teach him a trade?§ Is not labor a species of culture

---

* Abota, Chap, I.　　† Talmud Jerushalmi, Kiddoush, Chap. I.
‡ Middrash, Koheleth.　　§ Kiddoushim, Chap. I.

far preferable to indolent meditation?* Is it not necessary for our health, and does it not honor those who perform it.† And is not the very name sanctified by God who executed the *work* of creation.‡

But what finishes the picture, is the very example of the Pharisees, who humbled themselves to the lowest trades, and who thought neither their virtue nor holiness injured by making stockings for Roman courtezans who, debased though they were, but touched perhaps by that *Jewish magic* proscribed by the Senate, knew no oath more solemn than, *I swear by the life of the holy doctors of Israel's country.*§ The fact as to industry needs no long citations; if the history of the Pharisees prove anything, it is that trade or manual labor always accompanied their study of the Law. Was not Jesus a carpenter and Paul a tent-maker?

As in practical life we adopt some general maxims for starting points, so in all our actions we ought to have some final object in view. Of the first, we have spoken at the commencement of this work, where we gave those summaries of the law which were made the rules of conduct, but which, in the hands of Christianity, became completely void. Now, has Christianity any object to give us with which Pharisaism was not previously acquainted? Paul has given us the watch-word of which the Church has often made bad use, namely, the *glory of God*. With him all acts, however poor and mean, should have regard to the greater glory of God. "Whether you eat or drink, or whatever you do, let it be to the glory of God." We think we hear the Pharisees teaching the disciples: "In what little sentence of the Bible is the whole body of the Law enclosed?" In that from Proverbs which says, "In all thy ways remember God" (iii. 6);∥ that is, let all thy ways lead thee to and in God. Is not *unselfish worship* one of the oldest Pharisaical doctrines? "Be not as servants who serve their master for pay, but rather as slaves who serve him without hope of reward."¶ Is not this the worship that the Pharisees show us in Abraham, the patriarch of the Jews, and in Job, the patriarch of the Gentiles? Of the first it is written: "He loved God" (Is. xli. 8); the other cried: "Though He should kill me, I will put my trust in Him" (Job xiii. 15). Is not it in reference to such men that the Pharisees say: *They make peace for the family both above and below*;** that is, in heaven and earth? But it is not merely in religious or moral acts that we should keep this exclusive object in view. "Let all thine actions (ways) tend to the glory of God," says Rabbi Jose in the second chapter of Sentences from the fathers. And what an example Hillel presents! If he took leave of his disciples at meal-time, it was "*to*

---

* Talmud, Berachot, I. † Ibid, Gitten, VII. ‡ Gen. II, 2 Aboth of R. Nathan.
§ Ibid, Pesachim, 113. ∥ Ibid, Berachot, 63. ¶ Aboth, I. ** Sanhedrim, 99.

feed a poor man," and **when his** astonished disciples asked, "Has Hillel poor men to feed **every day**?" said : " It is this guest of a day, the soul, that I **must keep united** to the body." Whatever he did to the body **he used** to say, " I go to fulfil a precept." Entering the public baths, he said to his disciples : " Do you see those statues of the Emperor, with what care they are kept oiled and washed and preserved from injury? Well, do you not think we should do as much for this body, the image (Ikon) of the eternal King ?"* And is it in our actions alone that we should have this object in view? Jesus, true to the Pharisaical teachings, is more exacting : " I tell you that at the day of judgment men shall render an account of every idle word" (Mat. xii. 36). " The most trivial words even, exchanged between husband and wife, must be accounted for at the last judgment," say the Pharisees.† "Thou shalt converse about my commandments," says Moses ; *and not about vain things*, deduce the Pharisees.‡ David said : " Can ye (Judges), indeed, (if) *mute*, speak (expound) righteousness ?" (Ps. lviii. 1). And the Pharisees in comment : " What plan should man adopt in this world ? Let him be rather as a mute. For the Law too? No ; for as to that it is written, THOU SHALT SPEAK."§

Our theme is finished. Throughout this work we have, it will be noticed, quoted especially from the writings of the Pharisees and their maxims, showing the great part these played in the formation of Christian ethics. If the Bible, the Apocrypha, Philo, have been but rarely appealed to, is it because their replies would have been less favorable, less decisive? We think, on the contrary, that we could have had fine vantage-ground therefrom against our adversaries, and have much more easily and surely shown the superiority and anteriority of Jewish ethics to the Christian, from these sources. There are, doubtless, in the writings of the latter two—not to mention the Bible, wherein they abound—passages capable in themselves of curbing the whole of the evangelical ethics ; and Mr. Salvador has cited some very eloquent ones, though there were hundreds still. But many reasons led us to the choice we have made. The work we might have performed as to the Bible, the Apocrypha, and Philo, both Jews and Christians have done before us, and better than we could hope to do. These sources, especially the Bible, are much more accessible to all than are the almost unknown writings of the Rabbis. The ethics of the former Christianity will much more readily accept, as long as the Pharisees are regarded as the corrupters of Israel's ethics, and Jesus is believed

---

* Vayikra Rabba, XXXIV.   † Talmud, Chagiga, fol. 5.
‡ Ibid, Yoma, fol. 9.   § Talmud, Choullin, fol. 99.

to be its glorious restorer. In short, it the deplorable prejudices that have at all times hindered the due appreciation of Biblical ethics, are yielding daily to the advance of light and truth, they hold, alas! yet their old tyrannical sway over men as to the Pharisees. Consequently justice, truth, and the religious interests of the future forced us to examine what truth there is in opinions accredited at the outset and constantly fostered by that oldest enemy of the Pharisees, *Christianity*. Alas! we are forced to say that even among the valiant champions of Judaism, among the bold defenders of its morality we find no one who is not disposed, through some unaccountable condescension, to make enormous concessions, to sacrifice almost totally, the ethics, the rights, the reputation of Pharisaism, to the reigning system of morality, on condition that the rights of the Bible are preserved. With this mournful fact before us, it was reasonable to ask ourselves if actual Judaism, that which recognizes tradition as its guide, as the source of both its ethics and religion—if, in a word, Pharisaical Judaism ought to bow its hoary head to this creation of one of its own disciples, of the smallest of its children—the Benjamin of the school—and to own that if Jesus had not lived it would have been all over with the purity and spirit of Hebrew ethics. To answer this doubt, to end a perplexity that rendered modern criticism dumb, was this work undertaken; to see, in short, if religious Judaism has reason to envy that other historical and philosophical Judaism, which they have dressed up. We humbly confess that what we have given of the ethics of the Pharisees, of their ideas and maxims, forms but a very small fraction of the great riches, of the sublime thoughts that the Talmud, the Midraschim, the Zohar contain. Mixed throughout these books, in the most irregular manner with lore of all sorts, thoughts of wonderful beauty and elevation arrest the reader at every page. What we have cited will show, we hope, that the condemnation of the Pharisees cannot be a final one, that a new trial, a new judgment are indispensable, and that there has been too much *precipitation*, when, to fill up the gulf which separated the two religions, the Pharisees were cast in; the Pharisees, I say, who are truly rather the road, the bridge that criticism should preserve for both. After all we have said, we were grieved and surprised beyond measure to read the words with which Mr. Salvador seemingly desires to lead the way for the pretensions of Christian ethics.

According to him, the Pharisee doctors, "instead of dealing spiritually with the moral precepts of the Law, turned them into pure questions of civil right, hampered them with restrictions, multiplied subtleties; so that before their own exhortations could influence the mind, the heart had time to freeze and become insensible."

Mr. Salvador sees but one of the two parts played by the Pharisees. They were at once the *jurists* and the *moralists* of Judaism. To judge of their ethics when they speak *law* would be as just as to estimate their legislative skill by their ethical teachings. The double character of Judaism deceived Mr. Salvador. No soul in the ethics of the Pharisees! But what source more pregnant with emotions than this? What touching language; what accents, now pathetic, now terrible or sublime! We are moved with these venerable doctors we weep for their tears, we rejoice for their joy; the very play of their imagination, their legends and myths, have something simple, gracious, and child-like, that smiles upon us. No soul in the ethics of the Pharisees! Why if it have any defect, it is that it has too much; their emotion runs to tears, their plaints are like those of the dove, their pain like the roarings of the lion. This we cannot help seeing. The same illusion, the same inability to see in the Pharisees, the *moralists*, as well as the *jurists*, causes Mr. Salvador to add: "Being confined to the minutiæ of national and human interests, they took cognizance of external actions only." This, indeed, is monstrous. We must truly say that Mr. Salvador's first blunder in not recognizing the Mosaic system as solely a *policy* and not at all a *religion*, has brought about his strange contradictions to the best proven facts. One need not be as well versed as he in Hebrew knowledge to know that the Pharisees, *so far from taking cognizance only of external actions*, penetrated, on the contrary, into the most private recesses of the human heart, disclosing its weaknesses, its caprices, its most subtle artifices, and demanding purity of thought and sentiment, the curbing of our passions, just as well as obedience to the practical laws, civil or religious. If, performing functions so diverse as those of *legislators* and of *moralists*, they kept the law and ethics, each in its distinct and unchanging place, neither encroaching on the other—are they to be reproached by us (children of the 19th century) with this as a crime? Will Mr. Salvador cast the first stone at them for an act that constitutes their very glory? The same forgetfulness of the moral role of the Pharisees—of the charity that is one of the chief elements of Pharisaical Judaism, has dictated to Mr. Salvador the following words: "To the spirit of justice that shone in the doctrines and genius of Israel, Jesus added the no less precious qualities of sympathy and mercy. These old Pharisees would be astonished to learn that *mercy* and *sympathy* are the heritage of their young disciple, **they** who said, *The mercy and sympathy we enjoy with God are the reflection of the mercy and sympathy we enjoy with men;* they who have seasoned all their moral teaching with so much poetry, grace, and sentiment! No; in place of saying that Jesus adds to the Hebrew ethics mercy and sympathy, an impartial and courageous criticism would have said that he pays not sufficient regard to the spirit of justice.

Mr. Salvador has characterized the two ethical codes by a similitude that is not lacking in originality or truth. He says that the legislative and natural ethics of Moses is *man* in the full strength and expansion of his faculties ; that the ethics of Jesus is *woman*—woman with her sensibility, grace, and tender yearnings. One trait is wanting to these pictures to make them likenesses ; to both is wanting a stroke of the pencil that the whole face of each may be given. We shall not raise a petty dispute with Mr. Salvador about a *legislative ethics*, nor about a natural ethics ; we shall not say that to our view the first is as unintelligible as the second—if not more so. Nor shall we say that a natural ethics would possess essentially those very characteristics that Mr. Salvador says the Jewish ethics lacks, namely, passion, sentiment, and expansion. We shall only say that Jewish ethics indeed resembles *man*, but man in his double nature ; that is, the *primitive man* of Moses, the *androgyne* of Plato, the *bisexual man*, or rather, man and woman reunited by marriage; in a word, the *family home*. Yes, Christian ethics resembles *woman*, but woman isolated from man, without the counterpoise of his judgment, firmness, and experience ; woman, surrendered to all the impulses of sensibility, tenderness, passion, anger, in short, the *cloister*. Jewish ethics is justice and charity united, each tempering the other and both working in unison for the government of the grand family, mankind ; the one, having as its special organ, the *written law* ; the other represented rather by the *oral law* ; the one having to deal with society whose interests it governs, the other having its seat rather in the conscience of the individual. Thus Judaism includes the whole man, body and spirit, life actual and life to come ; the first coming from the Mosaic code, the second from tradition, which is the code of conscience. When Mr. Salvador ascribes to Judaism an exclusive worldly-mindedness, thereby contrasting it with Christianity that neglects the interests of this life for those of the next, he leaves out a whole side of Judaism ; this he makes err on the one side, and Christianity on the other ; he decides in favor of those who accuse Judaism of materialism, and accredits **the** prejudice that the *Jew* worships material interests—all for **not** bearing sufficiently in mind tradition, for not regarding Pharisaism **as** one phase of the Mosaic system rather than that system in **its entirety.** Had he been more orthodox he would have been less **assailable.** For us, Judaism is at once *justice* and *charity*, the **moral** law and the political **law,** the Mosaic code and tradition. The **one** is religion for the use of the nation, a collective being that **exists** in this world only (and hence its apparent materialism); the other is the code of conscience, the source of dogmas, principles and hopes that have reference to the **human soul** (hence its apparent asceticism). Both together constitute *Judaism*.

Is it not the same in dogma? Does not the family below (as say the Cabalists) reflect for us the family above. Have we not in dogma also a justice, which is the *Word*, and a charity, which is the *Kingdom*? And what completes the analogy is, that the first is called the *written* Law, the second the *oral* Law. Who can doubt that the Cabalists perceived the distinction and the different roles that we have indicated? Christian ethics is but *charity*, the celibate woman, the devotee, the nun, with all her virtues and vices, her delusions and passions; but as cabalistic *Charity*, separated from its spouse (the *Word*, *Justice*), is ruined by its very excess—being less than just through its being only charitable—so Christian charity, having rejected its natural comrade, justice, is condemned to assume the duty of the latter, no longer according to the fixed laws of justice, but after the impulses, the caprices of love and passion, that sometimes impose on their object what they ignorantly take to be salvation, glory, and happiness.

The way we understand the Jewish and the Christian ethics is this; instead of saying with Mr. Salvador that **the first is** *man*, the second, *woman*, **we say**,—the first is the conjugal state, the family, man in his entirety; the other **is a** *recluse*, a devotee, woman without the counterpoise of **husband**. And this too is how ethics, in its final consequences, connects itself with the speculative side of both religions—how *Ethics* is but *Dogma* **itself** presiding over the **government of** the conscience and the **destinies of nations.**

DOCTRINES AND ETHICS

OF

ISLAMISM

MOHAMMEDISM:

ITS DOCTRINE.

In an investigation of the influence that Judaism has had **upon** subsequent religions, we cannot but take notice of one other system which has left a deep and durable trace in human history—we allude to Islamism. The natural limits of the task we have undertaken, **as** well **as those of** the time at our command, compel us to restrict ourselves **to a narrower** circle than we should otherwise have kept. We do not, therefore, enter upon a general examination of Islamism, nor of the different theological or philosophical schools it has begot; we treat briefly only **of** that great branch which connects it with Judaism, and of its numerous and important **kindred** sprays.

Let us first take, from a suitable hight, a general review of this **religion**; let us ask what is the main impression it produces on the **mind of** an impartial observer; what are the links that connect it with Judaism, and, perhaps, with Christianity also.

We have proved, the reader will remember, that, **of** the two interests embraced **by** Judaism—the future life and the present one, or, (to use a Cabalistic expression) the *superior mother* and the *inferior mother*—Christianity selected exclusively the former, disdaining and neglecting the present life and its manifest concerns. Much more: **we** have seen how Christianity, when obliged to postpone the new resurrectional era it preached as impending, and to concern itself about the imperious needs of the present life, always subordinated those needs, and the interests of the actual world, to that fictitious, imaginary world of the resurrection, whither Christians thought themselves transplanted, in spirit at least, if not **in** body.

Judaism, ever mutilated, ever deprived of that element connecting **it** with this life, namely, of the body, the family, society, country; **of life,** in short, in all its various aspects! Ever the exclusive culture **of** the spiritual side of Judaism, of faith proper, of the individual conscience, in which man, despising the fore-named **relations of** the present life, **shuts** himself up and intrenches himself!

A phenomenon, just the reverse of this, awaits us in Islamism. It is the other side of Judaism, the one abandoned by Jesus, that Mahomet selects for his chief principle, for the corner-stone of his system.

If Jesus fastened on the most esoteric, the most spiritual doctrines of Judaism, bringing, from the depths of the sanctuary, the most abstruse metaphysics, to construct from it a religion for the million, imperiling, by the abuse of this esoteric theology, the very unity of God—that popular Monotheism which checked the flights of every audacious spirit—imperiling this, we say, by his theory of *persons*,— it is quite the opposite defect that we have in primitive Islamism.

The Arabian prophet—so little conversant with the rabbinical literature in which Jesus excelled, so far from Palestine and, above all, from that time and society of which Jesus was the product, when the Hebrew mind was in a state of ferment to find some central point of thought, when speculations jostled each other on all sides, and intellectual development had reached the zenith of power and productiveness—Mahomet could see only what struck every eye, what all could comprehend, what the Jews bore everywhere with them, viz, external Monotheism; and this, accordingly, was the solitary and supreme dogma of his religion. If Jesus took from Judaism its moral, interior and spiritual side, and thereby showed himself the disciple of the Pharisees rather than of Moses,—Mahomet, on the other hand, took from it its social and worldly side, and thereby attached himself to the Bible and to Moses rather than to tradition and the Pharisees. In short, if Christianity carried the principles and rules of a future life into the very midst of the present one, if it effaced and absorbed in the world to come the present world, imposing upon the latter the conditions of eternity,—it is precisely the antithesis of this doctrine which we get from Mahomet. He fashions and regulates the world to come after the model of our present life, whose pains, pleasures, passions, caprices, etc. he transfers to the future state, wherein is nought but a prolongation, a repetition of man's life here-below. Islamism, by excluding the spiritual side of Judaism, has barbarized its polity; Christianity, by soaring beyond the social life of Judaism, has transformed its religion into ascetism. In both cases is Judaism mutilated—deprived of one of its essential members.

This recognition, however, of the most striking characteristics of Mohammedism has, from our stand-point, a value, inasmuch as it implies some real and historical transplanting of Jewish doctrines into the new religion of Arabia. Are these grafts possible? The sequel will prove, we think, that they have actually taken place; the traces of Judaism, and of even Pharisaism will clearly appear in each detail, belief and precept of the religion of Mahomet, and in a manner so peculiar, so exact, as to leave no doubt possible. Now, let us see if external conditions and the relative situation of the Jews to Mahomet allow us to suppose this transplanting (incontestible in any case), and whether or not these relations be of a character to warrant such an hypothesis.

What do we see in Arabia, in the time of and close to the person of Mahomet? We see the Jews peopling in great numbers those countries where Mahomet's name was about to echo, and bearing with them that religion which, during their exile, is not to leave them again; and, what is much more, we see their credit constantly increasing, their influence and, therefore, their *religion* becoming dominant. History attests, in the most formal manner, that several princes and tribes embraced the religion of Israel. Mahomet now conceives his bold scheme of reform. Will he forget the potent aids that are within his reach? Far from it; as to Judaism, reckoning as it did so many adepts among Arabia's most distinguished children, he has nought but advances to make, and thinks he cannot treat with too much consideration those formidable rivals; he will adopt a great number of their opinions, their doctrines, their customs, seeking thereby to range them, if possible, on his side. Vain efforts! These faithful Israelites will never renounce one part of their religion, even though it were to see the other adopted by the prophet of Araby; and the world shall have a new religion modeled somewhat after Judaism, without this last ceasing to be what it has been, or that fountain being sullied at which other generations shall quench their thirst. Whatever results Mahomet may have expected from these Hebrew grafts, these have ever been recognized as such by every serious historian of Islamism. Has not an influence still more direct and continuous been brought to bear upon it! History tells us of the Jew Abdalla, who, as his secretary, was close to Mahomet's person, and who, if we mistake not, was authorized by the cotemporary Rabbis (as their books attest) to co-operate with Mahomet in the religious reform of Arabia. And who can say that the purity and elegance of style which is observable in the Koran and from which Mahomet takes an argument for his inspiration, have not flowed from a Hebrew pen? On this point, no weak testimony is that of Judaism's two great enemies, viz, of Christians and of Mahomet's cotemporaries. Now both recognized the hand of a stranger with Mahomet in the composition of the Koran, and it was, as Christians declare, that of the Jew *Abdalla*, and of the Monk *Sergius*. The Koran itself lends force to this opinion, entertained since the time of Mahomet. There are two passages in the book that allude to the point, and both testify equally, I think, in favor of Hebrew co-operation. In the 25th Chap. Mahomet exclaims, "The incredulous say: What is this book, but a lie that he has forged? Others, too, have helped him to make it . . . . . . they are but the myths of antiquity . . . . . he hears these things morning and evening." Could he so express himself respecting doctrines that were not of Jewish origin? And in Chap. 16th: "We know well the incredulous say: Some person teaches Mahomet. For the language of him whom they would impose on us is barbarian, and you see that the Koran is an Arabic book, clear and intelligible." Here the portrait becomes more definite and the Jewish type comes out more plainly. The doubt refers to some one who spoke a *barbarian tongue*. Now, who could this be but a Jew? A monk, even, could suit badly this portrait; for his language, ordinary or religious, would have always been Arabic, and nothing but Arabic.

Before entering on an examination of the doctrines and precepts of Islamism, let us mark, as we go, some circumstances in the life of Mahomet, evidently copied from Jewish history, either by Mahomet himself, an imitator and plagiarist of ancient narratives, or by his historians. The cave to which he retires, the choice which he makes of his twelve chief disciples, recall to mind, the one, the retreat of Moses and Elias, the other the choice of the twelve Princes of Israel, imitated by Jesus in the election of twelve apostles. But what especially attests the action of Pharisaical doctrine and tradition upon the history of Islamism is that spider that comes so opportunely to cover with his web the entrance to the cave to which Mahomet betook himself to escape the pursuit of the Koreish,—just as the Rabbis tell us how David was hidden from Saul, by a spider that spun his web across the entrance of the grotto, that David might be undeceived as to the uselessness of the spider, as he was, subsequently, at the Court of Achis, respecting the inutility of madness. And such a perfect harmony with the details of Pharasaical tradition is not the least proof that this is the model from which the anecdote of Mahomet's life is taken.

The doctrine and precepts of Islamism are contained chiefly in the *Koran*. Now, what is the Koran? This word is evidently derived from the verb *Kara, to read*, and therefore signifies, *reading, what ought to be read*, and is but an imitation of the word *mi-karah*, that Judaism has given to the Bible, each term being applied, severally to designate not only the whole sacred volume, but also, a section, a verse, or even a word of the special religion But the Jews apply other names still to the different parts of the Bible and of the Pentateuch, and that of *Parascha* (division) is one not the least ancient. Now, does not the Koran reproduce this appellation in the term *El Forkan*, (the divisions), taken evidently not only from the *Perek* or Pirka of the Rabbis, as Mr. Sale asserts, but from the analogous divisions of the Bible, called Parascha? And what, even are the *Sowars* or sections of the Koran but the *Sedarim* into which the Pentateuch is divided? Shall we esteem the other Arabic names of the Koran more original,—El Moshaf (the book), El Kitab* (the scripture)? They are but the translation of the Hebrew words *Sepher* and *Kitbe haccodesch*, applied to the Pentateuch, or to other parts of the Scriptures. The same precautions taken by the Rabbis to preserve the purity of Scripture have been adopted for the Koran, and the verses, words, letters even of the Koran, as of the Bible, have been counted, and they have likewise reckoned how many times each letter in the Koran occurs. Is not this pure Rabbinism? But this is not all. At the head of certain chapters of the Koran, we remark certain meaningless letters, the signification of which Mussulmen themselves do not know. Yet, how are they interpreted? In two ways, both equally Rabbinical, the *Notaricon* and the *Ghematria;* that is, by taking them at one time as the initials of certain words, and, at another, by calculating their numerical value, and supposing an allusion to other words of similar numerical value.

But, what to our view is most significant, is the idea Mahomedan orthodoxy entertains of the inspiration of the Koran,—one altogether analogous not only to what exoteric Judaism but to what the Cabalists teach on this subject—which strongly implies the existence of the Cabala in those remote times. The Arabs consider the Koran not only a divine revelation in the sense that it is the work of God, but in a more metaphysical one, namely, that the thoughts therein constitute the eternal mind of God, and are his word, his *Logos;* that they exist, as some say, in the divine essence; that the first copy of the Koran has been from all eternity at the throne of God, written on a vast table that contains his decrees as to the past and future. Is not this Hebrew doctrine uttered by the Arabs? Exoteric Judaism had been very explicit. "The Zorah," it says, is the model after which God "created the world; it is but one leaf dropped from the eternal wisdom, the instrument God used in his six days work." But how conclusive is the exoteric doctrine! We have already seen, when treating of Christianity, that the Hebrew *Verbum* is the written law, and that its spouse, *the Kingdom*, is tradition. But what is now very important to remark, is, that both these laws, scripture and tradition, the Verbum and the Kingdom, are identified in a higher degree in the scale of emanations, in that superior Wisdom called simply the eternal Law, *Tora Kedouma*. of which, when divided, the written and the oral Law are but the two parts. But the Arabian doctrine sees, in the eternal text of the

* Pure Hebrew also; the singular of *Kitbe*.

Koran, the "table of destiny." Is not this, word for word, what the Cabala teaches us? Is it not this same wisdom, this same eternal Law, which is called *destiny, fate*, although in a very different sense from the Mahometan fatalism? We can but glance at this subject now. Let those more favored than we extend this curious parallel; we shall be content to have broached the subject.

It is unquestionable that the doctrine we ascribe to the Arabs has ever been the most accredited among the orthodox; that if the sect of Montazales rejected it, from the fear of admitting two deities, it was from not well understanding this ancient doctrine, the true meaning of which Al-Ghazali has established in saying that if we speak what is contained in the Koran, if it is written in books and stored in the memory, it is nevertheless eternal, because it subsists in the essence of God from which it cannot be parted by any transmission to men.

If we ask what Islamism thinks of the interpretation of its holy writings, we shall find it to be exactly what the Pharisees and the Cabalists have taught respecting that of the Bible. Needless to say that they, too, carefully distinguish the literal from the spiritual interpretation. But what is noteworthy, is the image by which a celebrated Arab (El Jahed) distinguished these two senses of Scripture. He said that the Koran is a body which can change itself at one time into a man, at another into an animal, or, as others express it, that this book has two faces—one, that of a man, the other, that of an animal. Can we not see in this a trace of the old distinction made by the Psychics and the Pneumatics, between the different classes of the faithful and readers of the Bible—one just made by the Cabalists, and after them, as we have elsewhere noticed, by the Christians and Gnostics?

We lay no stress on the respect and veneration with which the Arabs regard their *books*. Every religion claims this from its adherents, and in this is no special trace of Judaism or its traditions. But must we not remark the use the Arabs have ever made of them? When some important occasion requires a decisive course of action, the Koran is consulted. The book is opened, and omens are taken from the first words that present themselves. Is not this what the oldest Pharisaism has done? We shall not speak of the custom of modern Jews. But the Talmud brings this mode of consulting the future as far back as the days of Josias, when it tells us of the terror of this King on reading in the Pentateuch, half opened by him, that prediction of Moses which condemns the King and the nation to exile, as a punishment for their sins.* The example of the Essenes, of which Joseph tells us, those of the Pharisees with which the

---

* Talm. Youma, fol. 52.

Talmud abounds, **prove** that omens were taken from verses of the Bible, read or **recited** by children, either spontaneously or by request.

But enough of the Koran, and of the opinion entertained respecting it by the Arabs. It is time we should speak of the contents of the book,—that is, of Islamism. This religion is divided by Arabic theologians into two parts, which give the essential elements of all religions,—the *Iman*, or the dogma, faith, theory,—and the *Din*, or the Law and its precepts. Islamism, as a whole, recognizes five main articles, of which only one belongs to the dogma, or *Iman*, the rest to the *Din*, or to worship and practice.

The former is the confession of faith which every Mussulman consider as the summary of his religion, viz: "There is no God but the true God, and Mahomet is his messenger." But this article includes six distinct elements: 1. Belief in God. 2. Belief in his angels. 3. Belief in his scriptures. 4. Belief in his prophets. 5. Belief in the resurrection and judgment-day. 6. Belief in the absolute decrees of God, and in the predestination of good and evil.

The four articles, including worship and practice, are: 1. Prayer. 2. Alms. 3. Fasting. 4. Pilgrimage to Mecca. Let us examine briefly, in succession, these articles of the Mussulman faith, and let us trace, if possible, that Judao-Pharisaical influence which we have already pointed out in the few preceding observations.

It will suffice here to recall what we have said respecting the unity of God, so prominent in Islamism, namely, that the doctrine is pure exoteric Judaism untempered by religious metaphysics, just as the Christian Trinity, on the other hand, is this very metaphysics, separated from what always controls its scientific march and development, namely, from popular monotheism. So that Judaism has been, if we may so speak, cut in two at the birth of its two children, each bearing away the half of its doctrine, and making of that half an exclusive creed.

The doctrine of the Koran as to angels is, that they have a pure and rarefied body, created by fire; that they neither eat nor drink; that they have no need of propagation by marriage; that they have different occupations and modes of serving God—some singing His praises; others interceding for the human race; others writing the actions of men; others carrying the heavenly throne. But the greatest of all are Gabriel (also called the Holy Spirit), Michael, the friend and protector of the Jews, Azrael, the Angel of Death, and Israfel, the trumpet-blower at the judgment-day. Have we not in this description the most marked traits of Pharisaical angelology,—nay, of the most special doctrines of Cabalistic Pharisaism?

That the bodies of angels consisted of an ethereal matter was one of the most characteristic opinions of this school; it was openly professed by a great number of the Church Fathers; it is, we will affirm, at the root of many systems of ancient or modern philosophy (above all as to what concerns the human soul, which they believed invested with a very subtile body). This body is a fire, according to the Psalms and the Talmud.* Each angel has one certain office, from which comes his name. Those who intercede for men are called Paracletin.† According to the Talmud, Elias writes down the actions of men; and, according to others, it is Gabriel who does this duty, as the prophet Ezekiel tells us, giving us all the marks of the scribe.‡ Need we say that the task of carrying the throne of God, assigned to the angels, is as old as this prophet himself? But we are obliged to go to the Cabala for information (to be sought for in vain in exoteric Judaism) respecting that quaternity of angels who preside over the whole celestial army, called in Islamism Gabriel, Michael, Azrael, and Israfel. Where find this, if not in the Cabala? It alone recognized these four archangels, who surpass all others in dignity and power, and who command the four cohorts of the Schechina, and the names of the first two are exactly the same as in the Hebrew creed. As to Azrael, no doubt it comes from the Azazel of Moses, the angel to whom God devoted the scape-goat on the day of Atonement—the Azael of the Talmud and the Zohar.§ Should the name of the last (Israfel) be a reminiscence of that ancient doctrine, that the world must end by a general combustion, as it arose from the same? The Hebrew root (*saraph*, to burn) leads us to think so. However that be, one stone evidently taken from the great Cabalistic edifice is the term Holy-Spirit given to Gabriel. How explain this singular identity in the doctrines? Is it not the *malkhout* that bears the name Gabriel? And is not this also called Holy-Spirit? Why then do not these names always go together, since they represent but one and the same being? We just now said that the Azrael of the Koran was probably the Mosaic Azazel. Is proof wanted? According to Mahomet the Devil (Eblis), bore before his fall the name Azazel. Is he not clearly the same as the Angel of Death, Azrael? True, two beings are formed from him, but is it not simply the doubling of the Mosaic angel (Azrael), while he fills his office, and Azazel under his primitive name, before the Fall?

And as to this Fall—how did it happen? Here, the Pharisaical ideas are made quite manifest. According to the Pharisees, the greatest of the angels was seized with a violent jealousy of man,

* Ps. civ. Talmud Chagiga, fol. 13, 14.   † Ib. Shabbath, fol. 32, and Baba Bathra, fol. 10.
‡ Ezekiel, ix.   § Tal. Yoma, fol. 67 and Zohar, sec. Bereshith.

MOHAMMEDISM—ITS DOCTRINE.

Adam, whom all **creatures** obeyed, and to whom the angels themselves ministered. He took the form of a serpent, seduced the woman, and was the cause of sin and death. Then the curse pronounced against the serpent, took effect upon man also, and he fell from his first splendor. According to Mahomet, "when God ordered the angels to adore Adam, all obeyed, except Eblis (the Devil); he, filled with pride, refused, and was counted among the ungrateful." But this is not all; before the creation of man, as well as after his fall, Mahomet comes as close as possible to the Pharisees. Their tradition speaks of God consulting the angels before the creation of man, and of their response eminently adverse to this creation. Now, is not this what we read in the second chapter of the Koran? The Pharisees mention the penitence of Adam, and especially the prayer he was to pronounce in honor of the Sabbath. Now the Koran says expressly that God taught Adam a prayer, and that He accepted his repentance.

Besides the angels, the Koran mentions an intermediate order of beings, whom the Arabs call *Djinn*, or genii. This classification is exactly analogous to the *Schedim*, whom the Pharisees admit. Their description is faithfully echoed by that of Mahomet. According to the Pharisees, they are similar to men in three respects; as to foodt propagation and death;* and this is, word for word, what Mahome, teaches. He divides them into the good and the bad, thinks they can be saved and damned, like men, and that his mission includes their conversion also. This is, in other terms, what the Pharisees say of the *Schedim*, keepers also of the law of Moses, who were surprised by men just as they were praying. From even the deepest strata of the rabbinical myths has Mahomet plagiarized, perhaps because the Pharisaism that surrounded and acted upon him was of that legendary character that entertains the people especially with wonderful stories.

After these remarks upon the Koran, and the mode of understanding it, we need say but little upon the second point of the Mussulman faith, belief in the Scriptures. Let us merely add, that besides the Pentateuch, the Psalms, and the Gospel which they receive just as do Jews and Christians (though believing these books to be much corrupted by both), they suppose anterior books to have existed, of which exoteric Judaism makes no mention, but which are forever celebrated in the mysterious doctrines of the Jews. Where, if not from this source, could Mahomet have learned that there were books such as that revealed to Adam (*Sifra deadam harischon*), those of **Seth**, Enoch and Abraham, books which the Koran speaks of as **having** existed, though thought now to be utterly lost? Now the

* Talmud Chagiga, fol. 16.

whole ancient Rabbinical library (except the Zohar) makes continual mention of those books. From the same source we think Mahomet took the belief in the inspiration of certain patriarchs as Adam, Seth, Heber, Enoch, who, by no means get this quality from the Mosaic writings, but receive it in some degree from Talmudical Pharisaism, and then still more from the Zohar and the Cabala where their inspiration is regarded as complete.

Before speaking of the last article of Arab faith, the resurrection of the dead, we shall say a few words about the state preceding that event. When one is laid in the tomb, two angels, Monkir and Nakir, examine him upon his orthodoxy and conduct. If the answers are satisfactory, the body is allowed to rest in peace and be refreshed by the air of Paradise; but if the answers are otherwise, the deceased is struck on the temples with iron rods, till his cries are heard from east to west. Then they press the earth upon the body, which is gnawed by ninety dragons. What Jew has not heard of the *Chibbout hakeber*, the *flagellation of the tomb*. When the angel of death sits upon the sepulchre, the soul enters the corpse and lifts it to its feet; then the angel examines the deceased and strikes him with a chain, half of iron, half of fire, so that at the first blow all the limbs are disjointed; at the second, the bones are destroyed; and at the third the body is reduced to dust and ashes. Is not this the picture that Islamism has copied for the use of the Arabs?

The state of the soul after its separation from the body, gives us a subject requiring still more study and thought. It is impossible not to recognize herein the ideas of the Cabala in their parabolic or legendary form, one which brought them within the comprehension of all and transformed them into a capricious mythology, fascinating for the imagination of the people. Let us see what they teach. There are, on this subject, divers opinions among the Arabs, but, when properly viewed, they are only so many symbols detached from the great body of Cabalistic symbolism, all bearing the truest stamp, and concealing under faces the most divers, one identical doctrine. According to some, souls keep generally near sepulchres; and this is what the Cabalists tell us concerning the *Nefesch*, which rarely leaves its body, and especially about the *Habala degarme*, "the breath of the bones," which never leaves it. According to others, souls are with Adam in the lowest heaven, those destined for Paradise on the right, and those for hell on the left. Is not this a paraphrase of the Cabalistic dogmas? For these inform us that all human souls are contained in Adam, some in his head, some in his arms, others in his breast, and so on; and especially that the last heaven, the *Velon*, *Malkhout*, is the seat of souls; the good on the right, the wicked on the left.

A third opinion of the **Arabs** is that the souls of the just are preserved in the water-founts *Zemzem*, those of the wicked in the pit *Brohut*. Is not this the same doctrine under another form, the symbolism of which is more precise and marked? This *Velon*, or *Malkhout*, bears the significant name *Beer* of living water, expressed in the history of the desert by "the wells of Miriam." But what is less known, though no less interesting, is that while the seat of the blessed is called *Beer*, its counterpart, the diabolic kingdom, the seat of the wicked, is called by the slightly different name *Bor*, *pit*, which is one of the names of hell. Can we have a closer, a more evident analogy? According to others, souls stay seven days near the tombs, though it is not known what then becomes of them. The Zohar tells us: "During seven days the soul comes and goes from the tomb to its house, and from its house to the tomb; after seven days the body remains as it is, and the soul goes where it goes."* This is not all. The Arabs have another opinion very strange and curious, but which is repeated with singular exactness by the Cabalistic formula. Understand, if you can, what the Arabs mean by saying that "souls are in the trumpet, at the sound of which the dead shall rise." But connect these words with the Cabalistic symbols, and how clear becomes the sense! We have but to remember that the *spirit*, the intellect proper, NESCHAMA, has its seat in the BINA, "the superior mother;" that this *Eon*, this Sephira bears as its most legitimate name, SCHOPHAR GADOL, "the grand trumpet;" and lastly, that at the sound of this trumpet the dead must rise. Were we not right in saying that these doctrines are the light-centre that explains the two greatest religious derivations—Christianity and Islamism?

It is time we should allude to the resurrection itself. Here Pharisaical analogies abound. The bone called *el-aib* or the coccyx, which, according to Mahomet, will remain incorrupt to the last day, as a seed or leaven to renew the whole body, is the same as the bone *looz* of the Pharisees, which is to play the same part on the resurrection-day. The rain of forty days, which Mahomet says will make bodies germ like plants, is the *dew* which the Pharisees say shall fall to revive the dust of the tombs, as the morning dew revives the flowers.

We shall say nothing of the signs that are to herald this great day—signs taken now from the Bible, now from the Doctors; of the marks that the faithful and the wicked shall bear on their faces, imitated from Ezekiel; of the Hebrew Messiah transformed by Islamism into Antichrist; of the irruption of the Yadjoudj and Madjoudj, the Gog and Magog of the Jews, with all the circumstances attend-

---

* Zohar, section Vaychi.

ing their advent given by Ezekiel; of the *triple* sound of the trumpet, modeled from all the official sounds of Judaism, always triple; of the kind of dress with which the dead shall rise from their tombs, and which the Talmud* had already assigned them, in the gracious parable of "the grain of wheat which is sown naked, and buds clad in splendid attire." But what should arrest us for a moment is the part the sun plays in this great day. The Pharisees had said: There is no Hell in the world to come, but the sun shall leave his sheath, burning the wicked and comforting the just. One of the great sufferings of the wicked, as Islamism in its turn teaches, will be a great sweat, produced not only by the great concourse of beings, but especially by the *nearness of the sun*, which shall then be distant only a MILE.† The just will be secured from this evil, dwelling "under the shade of the throne of God." It is impossible not to recognize in this the impress of Pharisaism. But a still more important analogy, is the justification which the soul and the body shall plead in that great day, each trying to shift the responsibility of its evil deeds upon the other. "O, Lord," the soul will say, "I received from thee my body, because thou didst create me without hands to seize anything, without feet to walk, eyes to see or ears to hear, until I entered into the body; that, therefore, thou shouldst punish eternally." And on the other hand, the body: "Lord, thou didst create me like a stick of wood, unable to use my eyes to see, or my feet and hands to act, until this soul came to animate me; then my tongue began to speak, my eyes to see, etc. . . . . . ; punish, therefore, this soul eternally." Is not this the question that Marcus Aurelius proposed to Juda the Holy, as the Talmud relates?‡ What is God's reply, according to Islamism? The same exactly as that given by Juda the Holy. Then comes the apologue of the blind man and the paralytic, who having got into the fruit garden of the King, excused themselves by alleging, each, his impotence. In their narration, as in ours, God puts the paralytic upon the back of the blind man, judges them and punishes them in this position. So astonishing a conformity of ideas and images between Mahomet and the Talmud could scarcely be due to chance.

We shall but name other ideas and images common to both religions. The books that will be produced at the last day, the scales

---

* Sanhedrim, fol. 90.   ‡ Ibid, fol. 91.

† Our readers may smile at this as an absurdity. Let them remember, however, that this describes an "evil" and abnormal condition of things; and secondly, that they should have little difficulty in accepting this, if they can credit the modern teaching that our sun is ninety-five million miles distant (and stationary!), and that our cumbrous earth is traveling at a speed (nearly twenty miles a second!) which, if true, would annihilate all animal life, at least on its surface.

in which actions will be weighed, the bridge of Hell over which men are to pass, belonged to Pharisaism long before they figured in the Koran.* But these images are too deeply founded in man's spiritual nature to derive an argument from them. What best merits our attention is rather whatever is arbitrary and capricious as to places, as to the duration and nature of rewards and punishments; for if a resemblance between the religions in such matters be shown, it must have great weight for an impartial critic. Now we can with confidence affirm that in these respects the conformity is most striking. If the Koran makes seven degrees in Hell, the Pharisees give it the same divisions;† if its custody is entrusted to angels, if the damned confess the justice of God's judgment, if their tortures consist sometimes in an excess of heat, sometimes in an excess of cold, if those tortures are to have an end,—these ideas are all in the most celebrated Pharisaical writings, with the exception of the last, wherein they give themselves the advantage and the copyist has deviated from his model. For while with the Pharisees the limitation of punishment is a general law, applicable to both Jews and Pagans, with the Mussulmen it is confined to believers, and eternal punishment reserved for infidels and idolaters.‡

Islamism is no less indebted to Pharisaism for its description of Paradise. The latter locates it in the seventh heaven, called *Araboth*, at the foot of God's throne, which the Cabalists designate by the Sephira, the exact Eon of Malkhout, called Throne of God, Paradise, and Gan Eden,—the seat, as we have said, of souls.§ Islamism teaches that Paradise is situated in the seventh heaven, immediately beneath the Throne of God; the pearls and hyacinths with which it is paved, its walls of gold and silver, its pomegranates, grapes, and dates, of exquisite taste and perfume, its viands, its birds all prepared, the silk robes which the earth shall produce, are all modeled from Biblical and Rabbinical descriptions. The future Jerusalem, the Paradise or celestial *kingdom* of the Cabalists, shall be, according to the prophets, full of these wonders; its pavements, walls and windows of silver, gold and precious stones. We read in the Talmud that an incredulous disciple saw with his own eyes angels cutting precious stones of an enormous size; and the Rabbinical legends tell us that the earth shall produce in the days of the Messiah cakes and silk dresses ready made. Nor are the rivers forgotten: These, Mahomet says, shall be of water, milk, wine and honey. Exactly what the Haggada, the popular legends of the

---

* Yalkout Shimoni, fol. 153, and Sanhedrim.
† Ibid. Shimoni, Eroubin, fol. 19, and Zohar, Vol. ii, Ch. xxv: 2.
‡ Ibid. Shimoni, fol. 86 and 116; Zohar, 11, 19; Eroubin, fol. 19.
§ Talmud Tanith, fol. 25; Chagiga, Ch. ii.

Pharisees, teaches.* One kind only, that plays a great part in esoteric Judaism and especially in the Zohar, is forgotten—viz, the rivers of balm. As a compensation, Mahomet promises his followers "girls with large black eyes," (Hour el-oyn), who may have a remote relationship to the *Alamoth* (virgins), a name given by the Cabalists to souls detached from their bodies.

But what recalls us, beyond dispute, to the Pharisaical sources is the idea that God will give the blessed strength to enjoy his favors, so that they shall not sink under them; a noble and pure idea as it came from the Doctors, but one which Mahomet has degraded to the grossest instincts of the Arab race. It would be, however, unjust to deny that Mahomet is better than his disciples; for if the enjoyments he promises them are such as a good man would not covet here-below, he has rewards which he esteems far above all sensual pleasures,—such as to view the face of God every evening and morning,—one for which (as Al-Ghazali remarks) all the other pleasures of Paradise will be forgotten.

To finish with the dogmas of Mahomet, we have but a word to say upon *predestination*, or the eternal decrees of God as to the fate of men and their works. Singular destiny of moral liberty! Without an asylum or assured protection in the midst of ancient Paganism, we might yet have thought that the products of that religion which said: "I put life and good, death and evil, before you,—choose then life,"† would have a little better respected *God's gift*, the power by which man most resembles his Creator. Vain hope! In the transmission of the Jewish dogmas to subsequent religions, the first that suffered and was sunk in the wreck of Judaism, was *free-will*, liberty. Is it then fated that the people who "struggled with God and with men,"‡ shall be the born-guardian of all liberties? Impossible to deny it: in Christianity, as well as in Islamism, by violent death or by lingering consumption, liberty has perished. The former stifled it softly, noiselessly, by dint of favors,—favors anticipatory, efficacious, irresistible, favors of every kind and shade, till liberty finally sunk under the weight of so many benefits. It was killed in the name of the *goodness of God*, which, nevertheless, never shone higher than when God, limiting man's power, yet said to him: *Be free!* Islamism, on the other hand, has killed it with a single blow, as its Califs and Sultans cut off heads with the cimeter; it has killed it in the name of *the knowledge of God*, which, nevertheless, is never so great,—of *his power*, which is never so powerful as when, superior to itself, it limits its own action.

Need we say that Pharisaism is free from these excesses? We say designedly, *Pharisaism, Judaism;* for none other has kept the proper

* Yalkout Shimoni.   † Deut. xxx: 15—19.   ‡ Gen. xxxi: 9.

mean in this grave problem. On one side, the Sadducees, as Joseph attests, set no bounds to human liberty,—a system as absurd as it was impious. On the other, the Essenes spoke a language in which contempt was almost inevitable. They ascribed (Joseph still our witness) all to destiny.

Far from us the thought of seeing in the *destiny* of the Essenes the *fatalism* of the Mussulman or the *necessity* of Spinoza. But without being the cause, it has assuredly given occasion to the second, and perhaps also to the first. We should, however, for the honor of the human mind, much more than for that of Islamism, remark that the Arab philosophy has struggled in every way against the evil consequences of the fatalism consecrated by Mahomet, and that it has been sometimes bold enough to maintain the opposite opinion,—to assert that the free judgment of man is intact.

CHAPTER II.

WORSHIP AND ETHICS.

The examination we have made of the Mohammedan faith has met our expectations. The result has but more and more demonstrated that Pharisaical origin which we strongly suspected from the first. A new study now presents itself, viz: The religious practice and worship of Islam. This, as we have said, includes four divisions: *prayer, fasting, alms and pilgrimage to Mecca*. Let us commence with prayer, but as this must be preceded by purifications, let us first say a word as to these. They are of two kinds: 1st, total purification, called, ghosl, that is, ablution of the whole body, corresponding to the Hebrew *tebila*; 2d, purification of the face, hands and feet, done after a set fashion, the *wodon*.

Here is a distinction corresponding exactly to the most ordinary practices of the Pharisees. Let us see if the mode of performance in Islamism be less simple. After sexual intercourse the whole body is to be purified by immersion; likewise, those who have been near the dead, and women who have been confined or have had their courses. These four cases are anticipated by Moses; but what best proves the Pharisaical derivation is the first ablution, which, though clearly enjoined by the Mosaic text, acquired its general signification and importance only from Ezra and the Rabbinical institutions. In short, the face, hands and feet are purified before prayer. It is true that this particular intention and special object did not enter into the rabbinical prescriptions; but the daily occurrence of the practice, and the general ideas of not approaching holy things without this purification leave no room to doubt that the same spirit presided in both cases regarding the object of these ablutions.

Still more,—the Pharisees, when water cannot be had, fulfil this obligation by using fine sand or dust, and to the same expedient, in a similar lack, has the Koran recource.

Although the Koran does not order-circumcision, the custom is too well known and too old among the Arabs to need mention. But what we should notice is that the Arabs say circumcision is as old as Adam, to whom it was taught by the angel Gabriel. Now, is not this, in another guise, the assertion of the Rabbis, that not alone was Adam created *perfect;* but many other Patriarchs after him were born circumcised.

Is this the only bodily preparation which the Arabs think indispensable to worship and prayer? The attitude of the body during prayer is no less necessary to render it acceptable. To turn towards the holy place is an indispensable duty, and all can see how the thought of Mahomet, and the ancient usage of Israel (practised by Daniel himself at Babylon) curiously coincide. How then, if we knew, for instance, that, according to the oldest injunction of Mahomet, it was towards Jerusalem one should face during prayer? But this fact is well established. Ever, even since Mecca has taken the place of Jerusalem, do Mussulmen and Jews at the hour of prayer, turn their eyes and bodies to their sacred cities.

Alms, the second precept of Islamism, is of two kinds, viz: legal and voluntary. The first is determined by law, regard being had to both the quantity and quality of the gifts; the other is left to the disposition of each, which is more similar to the Judaic institutions? In the latter also, we have tenths of all kinds, the corners of the fields, the small grapes or the forgotten corn-ears that belong in full right to the poor, to strangers, widows and orphans; and there is also the alms proper which each gives according to his means or generosity. The analogy appears already in this general distinction, and it is no less visible as to the time most suitable for the exercise of this duty. The Koran, as do the Rabbis, recommends the giving of alms at prayer-time, that it may intercede with God for us. We seem to hear and see Rabbi Eliezer, who always gave alms before prayer, recalling the verse from the Psalms: "I shall see thy face through charity."* Mussulman humanity extends to animals. Has it surpassed the sensibility and goodness of the

---

* Chap. xvii, 15—Talmud Baba Bathra, fol. 10.

Pharisees? Long before societies for the protection of animals were thought of, those Pharisees, so little known, declared that to give an animal pain is a sin against the law of God; and had Malebranche been a Jew he would not have given his dog that famous kick, saying: "She has no feeling." "The sophistry" of these Pharisees could discover in the most revered passages of the Pentateuch, the obligation to provide for the wants of animals before sitting to table, and one of these heartless, stupid Pharisees could eat nothing before ordering his oxen to be fed.*

The law of Mahomet prescribes nothing as to the quantity of alms. A new homage, as all can see, to the Pharisaic origin. Ordinary alms is generally confined to the fortieth part. This was the maximum which the Rabbis appointed for the *Terouma*, or tax for the sacrifiers. On extraordinary occasions, after gaining a battle or lucky speculation, very liberal alms should be given. What limit did Islamism prescribe? The very same as did the Doctors assembled at Ouscha to check the inconsiderate impulse of Hebrew charity—viz, a fifth.†

As to the third article of the faith, viz, fasting, Mahomet has exaggerated its value far beyond that given it by the Rabbis; perhaps because it appeared to him more meritorious in a people still subjected to the appetites of the flesh. Mahomet, however, seems to have taken one idea from the Rabbis when he says: "The breath of the faster is more pleasant to God than the odor of musk." Substituting the odor of *sacrifices* for that of *musk*, we have an imitation of the Talmud,‡ and especially of the Cabalists. How do Mussulmen keep the ordained fast, and what are the self-imposed privations? The Bible speaks but of the "affliction of the spirit," or rather of the mortification of the senses. But the Pharisaical definition gives us exactly the manner in which the Arabs keep the fast. To eat, drink, wash, annoint the body, or have sexual intercourse, are all forbidden by Jewish tradition during the great fast. And these acts the Koran likewise prohibits, from day-break to sun-set. If not abstained from, the fast is considered void. Day-break is the commencement of the Mussulman fast; but the Koran brings us still more closely than by this point to prove Pharisaism when it says that the fast commences as soon as a white thread can be distinguished from a black one in the light of dawn. This is what the Mischna lays down as to the reading of the Schema in the morning, viz, *as soon as blue can be discerned from white*. Mahomet designates the tenth of the month Moharram as the most appropriate day for fast. Does he but sanction a custom already in force among the Arabs, as Al-Ghazali thinks? We think it much more likely that

---

*Talmud Berachoth, fol. 40.   † Ib. Kethuboth, fol. 50.   ‡ Ib. Berachoth, fol. 17.

he has imitated the great Jewish fast on the 10th of the 7th month, especially as he too calls his fast *aschour* after the Mosaic *assor*, held on the day of Atonement.

As to the pilgrimage to Mecca, although Mahomet preserved a custom already in vogue among the Arabs, he has but followed the example of Moses, who enjoins on all Isrealites to visit the temple of God three times a year. If Mahomet has not been so exacting, and commands the performance of this duty once only in life, it is because his religion, like Christianity, was destined to spread itself wherever the sword or proselytizing opened a way, because it is much more a cosmical than a national worship, and because three annual visits to the temple at Mecca would have been almost impossible for the inhabitants of most countries. In giving precepts to the Arabs, Mahomet did not confine himself to purely positive ones, such as those we have mentioned. He forbid many things, of which we shall mention but two, where the imitation from the Jews is incontestable, viz: the use of certain meats, and usury. If the flesh of swine was rejected by the Arabs before Mahomet's day, as is pretended, no doubt that Mahomet himself forbid many other meats. Not only is pork forbidden by the Koran, but also blood, as well as all animals that die naturally, or that have been strangled, or slain by other animals; although all such are allowed under the pressure of imperious necessity, from want of food, or in extreme danger. Are not these purely Hebrew importations, both the precepts and restrictions?

Let us now take a rapid glance at the civil institutions of Mohammedism. Here it is that the Pharisaical influence shows itself in all its strength. Let us begin with *marriage*. The Koran allows polygamy. Is it as arbitrary and unconditional as some authors think? Far from it; the Koran is precise thereupon: no one can have more than four wives,—the exact number appointed by the Rabbis. The same causes that authorize, in Judaism,[*] a woman to demand a divorce, are equally admissible in the Mahomedan law, viz: bad treatment, neglect to maintain, impotence, or any other lack of conjugal duty. In both religions, a widow or repudiated wife, must wait three months before re-marrying; if she suckles a child, she must wait two years reckoning from its birth.[†]

Adultery in both religions is punished by stoning. To prove the crime four witnesses are required by Mahomet, two by Moses; and what deserves attention is the imprecation which the former imposes on a woman accused three times by her husband of adultery, obliging her, if she wishes to be acquitted to invoke the ven-

---

[*] Talmud Kethuboth, Ch. v—Shoulchan **Arouch**, Vol. iii, Ch. xiii.
[†] Maimondes Hitchouth Ishouth, xix.

geance of God on her head, if she is guilty. Is not this the imprecation accompanying the test of the bitter waters found in the book of Numbers?

The law of Moses does not allow human life to be estimated at a price. Murder must be punished, but not by a fine. Mahomet has greater flexibility. A compensation paid the family, the redemption of a captive Mussulman, will acquit the homicide, provided always the nearest relative of the slain is satisfied; otherwise, the criminal is given up to him to suffer any death such relative choses to inflict: a new lapse from the law of Moses, in which Mahomet falls into an excess of severity, as he just before erred by an excessive indulgence. Never did the law of Moses place the life of a man at the disposition of another; and if certain expressions seem to justify doubts on this point, it is because the nearest relative played, in Jewish society, the part of public accuser, and because putting the killer into the hands of *goel haddam*, means simply, surrendering him to his fate, public justice never foregoing its judgment or the execution of the criminal. Some would have it that the banishment of an unintentional homicide, ordered by Moses, was to save him from the anger of the nearest relative of the slain, and some have talked of the *spirit of vengeance* common to both Arabs and Jews, which originated the severe punishment in vogue with both. The Mosaic text in no wise justifies this interpretation, for the law as to involuntary homicide has all the marks of a public penalty, far more than those of a provision to defeat the revenge of relatives; and especially because an involuntary sin, such as the eating of blood or tallow, equally requires an expiation, and that by a sacrifice. But all suppositions of this kind crumble before Pharisaical tradition, which, far from extending this law, as the text might imply, to all involuntary killing, limits its action strictly to a homicide who kills through culpable negligence, and declares all others free to come and go without having to fear reprisals of any sort from the relatives.

The law of *retaliation* is sanctioned by the Koran as well as by the law of Moses; but what completely justifies the Pharisaical interpretation of this law is the Mussulman practice and interpretation of it. The Pharisees, as we know, assert that Moses' "eye for eye, tooth for tooth," etc., means only that their value shall be paid by *fine*. See how these "slaves of the letter" can foil an unjust and barbarous usage,—and see the services that Pharisaism has rendered humanity! Is it by a felicitous faithlessness to the Mosaic thought that they evaded the consequences of the literal interpretation, or have they taken liberties with the true spirit that dictated this law? One might think so, taking only the words of Exodus. But besides the significant phrase in Leviticus (Chap. xxiv: 18), one the most favorable for the Pharisaical exposition, the example of Islam is very noteworthy. Retaliation is there sanctioned in the same terms and with the same force as in the Pentateuch, and yet, strange to say! this law gets specifically the same interpretation as does the Mosaic one at the hands of the Pharisees. No doubt whatever; and seldom or never is the practical application diverse.

War upon infidels is one of the most sacred duties recommended by Islamism. The greatness of the reward promised to him devoting his time, fortune and life to this work, is equaled only by the punishment in store for those who refuse it their properties or persons, and for runaways and deserters. With Islam the sword is the key of heaven and hell, and those wars being religious could have no limits but those of the world swayed by the **Koran**. What **were** the holy wars for Christianity but religious wars? **Is** there anything similar in Judaism? Remarkable fact! Judaism, *nation, state, government* though it was, took good care not to enlist the state, the nation, in the service of its dogmas; through fear of raising a religious war, it condemned itself to wage no war, that is,—to be forever politically inferior; it forbid itself all aggrandizement, all conquests except what God had previously determined, and those in very modest measure. What a difference between the two doctrines! The sword, for Islamism, is the key to heaven and hell. **But for** the Pharisees, it is not merely no *ornament*, but an impure object that defiles the touch like a dead body.* Is this the spectacle with which the two religious offshoots of Judaism present us? In these no state, no nationality, no country—in short, no excuse—that might make a war more necessary, more lawful. They could have claimed, at less expense than could Judaism, merit for moderation, for love of peace. But nothing of the kind. In both cases, the *infidel* was the true *enemy;* what the word *barbarian* signified for paganism, what the political enemy was for Judaism, the *infidel* was for the Christian Church and for Islam, that is, their natural and proper enemy, the only enemy with whom they might have truce, but never a definite peace as long as he continued in his errors. No need for these sects to repeat the priests harangue to the people before battle,† or the words of Maimonides inspiring every Hebrew citizen‡ with courage for battle. There will ever be between a Hebrew war and a Christian or Mohammedan one, the difference we have named,—one as great as between the religions themselves—that abyss in short which men have made between them. The first one will never be more than a *defensive* war, or at most a political one; the other two are but and can be only wars of religion.

* Talmud Shabbath, fol. 63.   † Deut. xx: 2.   ‡ Maimon. Hilchouth Melachim, Ch. vii.

www.ingramcontent.com/pod-product-compliance
Lightning Source LLC
Chambersburg PA
CBHW030436190426
43202CB00036B/1372